Praise for *Spirit Conjuring for Witches*

"The call of the spirits is growing louder and louder and more people are answering that call by researching, re-creating, and creating new methods to conjure them. *Spirit Conjuring for Witches: Magical Evocation Simplified* by Frater Barrabbas is an orderly and detailed exposition of a clear and distinct body of tools and rituals for working with a broad range of spirits. If you are a witch looking for a more formal approach to this field, this may be the book for you."

—Ivo Dominguez Jr., author of *Spirit Speaks*
and *Practical Astrology for Witches and Pagans*

"In *Spirit Conjuring for Witches: Magical Evocation Simplified*, Frater Barrabbas has made a valuable contribution to the practice of modern witchcraft. The use of conjuration was, as he says, fundamental to traditional witchcraft practice and the witch of legend alike, yet conjuration is almost never practiced in contemporary Wiccan covens…What Fr. Barrabbas has most impressively accomplished is translating the necessary functions of this essentially 'reverse exorcism' out of the unsuitable Abrahamic preconceptions of the grimoires and rendered it accessible to modern pagans—no small achievement."

—Jim Baker, author of *The Cunning Man's Handbook*

"Frater Barrabbas shows how modern Witches can also reclaim their ability to conjure spirits in the age-old tradition of evoking beings of the Otherworld to attain knowledge or obtain practical results in this world. With the current revival in the publication, study, and use of the classical grimoires, witches who are drawn to the practice of the magickal evocation of spirits now have a detailed guide to the inner preparations and outer practices necessary to evoke spirits safely and correctly."

—Jonathan Nightshade, Gardnerian HP,
Traditional Crafter and Sorcerer

"I wish that there had a book like *Spirit Conjuring for Witches* back when; it would have saved me any number of missteps along the way. With more than forty years of experience under his cincture, Frater Barabbas speaks with a voice of wisdom, clarity and authority: truly one of the Thirteen Human Treasures of Paganistan."

—Steven Posch, Traditional Witch and Host of Radio Paganistan

"As Witches we all work with Deity and various spirits; but can you honestly say you communicate with them? This book is a valuable resource for every serious Witch's library. The author has outlined how to truly connect with that spirit realm, which allows us to build a relationship with those we work with."

—Lady Adariana, Gardnerian HPS

Also by Frater Barrabbas

Magical Qabalah for Beginners

Paul B. Rucker

About the Author

Frater Barrabbas (Twin Cities, MN) is a practicing ritual magician who has studied magick and the occult for over thirty-five years. He is the founder of a magical order called the Order of the Gnostic Star, and he is an elder and lineage holder in the Alexandrian tradition of Witchcraft. Visit his blog at fraterbarrabbas.blogspot.com.

To Write the Author

If you wish to contact the author or would like more information about this book, please write to the author in care of Llewellyn Worldwide, and we will forward your request. Both the author and the publisher appreciate hearing from you and learning of your enjoyment of this book and how it has helped you. Llewellyn Worldwide cannot guarantee that every letter written to the author can be answered, but all will be forwarded. Please write to:

Frater Barrabbas
℅ Llewellyn Worldwide
2143 Wooddale Drive
Woodbury, MN 55125-2989

Please enclose a self-addressed stamped envelope for reply,
or $1.00 to cover costs. If outside the USA, enclose
an international postal reply coupon.

Many of Llewellyn's authors have websites with additional information and resources. For more information, please visit www.llewellyn.com.

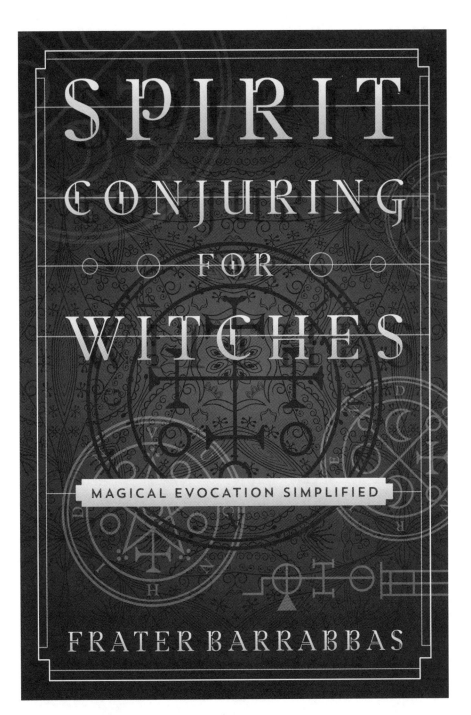

SPIRIT CONJURING FOR WITCHES

MAGICAL EVOCATION SIMPLIFIED

FRATER BARRABBAS

Llewellyn Publications
Woodbury, Minnesota

FIRST EDITION
First Printing, 2017

Book design by Bob Gaul
Cover design by Kevin R. Brown
Editing by Laura Graves
Figure 1 by Sara Joseph
Figures 2–9, 11–13, 15–18 by Llewellyn art department
Figures 10 & 14 courtesy of Liam Quin at www.fromoldbooks.org
Figure 19 by Mickie Mueller

Llewellyn Publications is a registered trademark of Llewellyn Worldwide Ltd.

Library of Congress Cataloging-in-Publication Data
Names: Barrabbas, Frater, author.
Title: Spirit conjuring for witches: magical evocation simplified /
Frater Barrabbas.
Description: First Edition. | Woodbury: Llewellyn Worldwide, Ltd, 2017. |
    Includes bibliographical references and index.
Identifiers: LCCN 2016043854 (print) | LCCN 2016048871 (ebook) | ISBN
    9780738750040 | ISBN 9780738751160 (ebook)
Subjects: LCSH: Witchcraft. | Magic.
Classification: LCC BF1566 .B264 2017 (print) | LCC BF1566 (ebook) | DDC
    133.4/3—dc23
LC record available at https://lccn.loc.gov/2016043854

Llewellyn Worldwide Ltd. does not participate in, endorse, or have any authority or responsibility concerning private business transactions between our authors and the public.

All mail addressed to the author is forwarded, but the publisher cannot, unless specifically instructed by the author, give out an address or phone number.

Any Internet references contained in this work are current at publication time, but the publisher cannot guarantee that a specific location will continue to be maintained. Please refer to the publisher's website for links to authors' websites and other sources.

Llewellyn Publications
A Division of Llewellyn Worldwide Ltd.
2143 Wooddale Drive
Woodbury, MN 55125-2989
www.llewellyn.com

Printed in the United States of America

Contents

*This book is dedicated to Kevin Wilson,
the witch who inspired me to write it;
to my dear wife, Joni, who taught me how to write
nonfiction and who has steadfastly supported my
writing endeavors; and to my beloved first cat, Jynx,
who passed away to Summerland last spring.*

Acknowledgments

I would like to thank Jim Baker for his invaluable help with the history of magic and witchcraft, and Steve Posch, for his steadfast support for my book project, and my close Witch friends who got to add their own two cents.

I would also like to thank Sara Joseph for her graphic and artistic help with producing examples of some of the illustrations.

Legendary Witches
and Their Craft

*I myself have seen this woman draw the stars from the
sky; she diverts the course of a fast-flowing river with her
incantations; her voice makes the earth gape, it lures the
spirits from the tombs, send the bones tumbling from the
dying pyre. At her behest, the sad clouds scatter;
at her behest, snow falls from a summer's sky.*

CATULLUS

We all know about the legendary witches who lived long ago in the
times of myth and magic, and we know them from our childhood when we eagerly listened to our parents read to us the timeless
fairy tales collected by the Brothers Grimm and others. We shivered
with delight hearing about how wicked they were and cheered when
they finally came to a bad end, vanquished by the stout-hearted hero or
some clever ruse. Some of us might have wistfully hoped that the witch
might live to see another day and maybe introduce another thrilling

story, or perhaps, like myself, they might even have felt sympathy for the wicked witch or sought to emulate her in some manner. Needless to say, most of us gave up our imaginative childhood for the rigors and seriousness of adulthood. The stories, legends, and myths receded into the fond and distant memories of our childhood as we took upon ourselves the trials, joys, and heartbreak of mundane existence.

We have left behind these legends, stories, and myths even as we pursued seemingly corollary paths such as Paganism and Modern Witchcraft. However, while we are pursuing a life that has only the remotest relationship to the color, vibrancy, and fascination of our childhood imaginings, the very stories that thrilled us as children have a powerful element of truth hidden deep within them. Even as we learn to master all of the modern tropes of Traditional Witchcraft, the very stories of the past starkly contrast to our self-conscious attempts at developing and promoting a new Pagan and magical-based religion. We are a pale and vaporous shadow when compared to the stories of the legendary witches and their associated powers and abilities. Of course we can scoff at these tales and relegate them to the fantasies of our childhood, telling ourselves that the real world requires a factual approach to magic and religion. The irony of this approach is that it is like the steadfast rationalist who whistles in the dark when walking past a graveyard at night.

This brings us to ask the really important question about all of our current achievements with Modern Witchcraft and magic: "Have we forgotten something important?" Is it relevant to compare ourselves to the legendary witches of the various myths and stories? Some might say that it is certainly not relevant (after all, we live in a modern world with obvious limitations), but I am one who thinks it is relevant. I believe that of all of the powers and abilities that the legendary witches possessed, it was their ability to conjure spirits and converse with them that was most intriguing. I found nothing in my Book of Shadows that formalized the methodology for spirit conjuring, and I have an authentic third-generation Gardnerian Book of Shadows, as does anyone who is in my line of Alexandrian Witches. Alex Sanders supposedly experimented with these and many other techniques, but it appeared he had only purloined his lore from what remained of the old grimoires of the previous epoch. Nothing was really passed down, so it seemed that such techniques were the provenance of ceremonial magicians.

That brought me to research some of the aspects and elements of the ancient witches, and particularly their ability to formally conjure spirits. I was particularly fascinated with the Old Testament Witch of En-dor who conjured the ghost of the prophet Samuel for King Saul because Yahweh had abandoned him. Like many witches from legends and stories, the Witch of En-dor had a familiar spirit (called in Hebrew an *ob*) that acted as her spiritual emissary for conjuring and divining. She was able to quickly evoke the ghost of Samuel when Saul requested, and the familiar spirit was the key to her having this ability. Other stories and legends from antiquity also attest to the fact that the conjuring witch had a familiar spirit to assist her in performing conjurations. So from the standpoint of a recurring pattern, we can safely assume that this was an important part of magical conjuration in the old days. It would likely also be relevant today but in a somewhat different manner, as we shall see.

Ancient and legendary witchcraft could be divided into five basic categories, and it is likely any true practitioner in those times would have been proficient in many but a master in only one. It also seems to be the case that these categories could merge with each other, but I think they represent distinct categories of capabilities. The categories are: thaumaturgy, potions making and herbalism, divination, spirit conjuration, and theurgy. Let us briefly examine each.

Thaumaturgy (wonderworking)—Thaumaturgy is defined as a nonreligious form of magic that uses the law of similarity (like affects like) and/or the law of contagion (once in contact, always in contact) to create talismans, amulets, curse tablets, voodoo dolls, and so on. This was probably the most common form of witchcraft magic (particularly if the objective was to harm someone), but it could also be used to positively impact or even heal someone or some creature. Common people knew how to perform some of these kinds of magic, and typically the purveyors of such trinkets and minor marvels were itinerant magical tradesmen. Less typical was the miracle worker. Forms of casting illusions (individual or mass hypnosis), legerdemain, automata, ventriloquism, and reading facial and body cues were also part of this kind of magic.

Potion making and Herbalism (*pharmakeutai*)—The potion maker was the prototype for the modern pharmacist, and many were quite proficient and knowledgeable of their craft. A person could purchase a remedy that contained real medicines in their raw form to heal the sick or poisons to stealthily murder an enemy. Real science was mixed with magic and quackery, but the results were often quite effective. One of the Latin names for a witch was *venefica*, "woman poisoner," so the potion maker was sometimes considered a witch. Later on, the legendary witch was often seen making large potions in a bubbling cauldron, like the three witches in the play *Macbeth*. This kind of magic is still quite relevant in the workings of Hoodoo and root work.

Divination—A diviner or sybil was someone who could, through using various auspices or manipulating divinatory tools, foretell the future. Some divination was sanctioned by the state (such as the oracle of Delphi in ancient Greece), and these were the various established oracles and regimented auspices where the deities could reveal their will through rather obscure and oblique declarations. There were also astrologers, clairvoyants, and many other unsanctioned diviners and soothsayers who used various tools and techniques to predict the future. Some of these diviners could be witches and sometimes spirit conjuring was employed, but I have confined that ability to its own category.

Spirit Conjuration—A conjuror was at the high end of magical ability, as she had the ability to intercede with various spirits and ghosts that resided in the spirit world. She likely had the ability to enter into that world herself and was able to mitigate the hauntings of restive spirits of the dead and give them peace. She could also stir up the dead, or raise the ghost of one's ancestors for nearly any purpose. She used this mechanism to acquire knowledge unavailable to anyone else, but she could also manipulate or enchant others and employ spirits or demons to do her bidding. She often represented (as a priestess) chthonic deities and made offerings to them, but seemed to answer to no known authority. Of the various practitioners she was one of the most dangerous. She typically had a spirit helper or assistant (familiar spirit) to aid in these tasks.

In antiquity, the word "witchcraft" was synonymous with another word, *goeteia*. The *goetes* were itinerant vagabonds in ancient Greece who acted as intermediaries between the living and the dead. Through their keening, moaning, and shrieking incantations, they could summon the unsettled ghosts and lay them to rest.[1] The goetes were typically considered charlatans and disreputable con artists by the philosophers of the time, but they were also in continual use by all classes of people living in Greece. Some of their remarkable legendary feats were considered quite amazing. It is likely that the conjuring witch and her methodologies in antiquity came from this tradition.

Some witches in antiquity were reputed to have godlike powers. This was due to the fact that they were the offspring of deities themselves and

---

1   Daniel Ogden, *Greek and Roman Necromancy* (Princeton, NJ: Princeton University Press, 2001), 100–102.

therefore had innate preternatural abilities to focus and use supernatural powers. This is where we encounter the great demigod witches in the tales and legends of antiquity, with such names as Circe, Medea, Erictho, or Canidia. These were women whose abilities were truly miraculous simply because they were the scion of gods themselves, having the power to change material reality at a whim. Such terrible and fascinating women were the inspiration for Catullus's poem cited at the beginning of the chapter. However, this ability was considered a special case for those who had such a supernatural pedigree. For everyone else, a spiritual intermediary was required because it was commonly believed that humans did not have innate supernatural powers.

Theurgy—Literally, "god work." While theurgia was represented as the high art belonging to the philosopher in the task to gain all knowledge of things spiritual and material, this magical technique was also performed by individuals who were reputed to have godlike powers, such as Apollonius of Tyanna. It was a system of practice and study that allowed mere humans to aspire to ascend and become like the gods, even though this was more often an ideal that was rarely attained. Modern writers of magic, particularly those since the post-Enlightenment period, have redefined theurgy to amplify the human potential in accordance with more modern perspectives about the innate possibilities available to all human beings.

A more typical kind of magic used by nearly everyone in association with the gods consisted of invoking one of the deities for the purpose of coercing or bribing them to perform a task. This could be as simple as making votive offerings, sacrifices, special paeans, and invocations to a direct approach by invoking, commanding, and summoning the deity. Antiquity is full of these kinds of operations, and they are not so foreign to us today—particularly to the many practicing Catholic or Orthodox Christians. What might seem a bit extreme today is that some of the ancient practitioners had the ability to direct and coerce the gods to do their bidding. This is still done in some situations using the icons or reliquaries of saints in outlying Catholic and Orthodox churches, but it would be considered bad form to try to directly coerce God.

The aforementioned methods of ancient witchcraft can be found in some form or another in Modern Witchcraft except for conjuring spirits. Modern witches perform thaumaturgic spells, make herbal concoctions and medicines (similar to Hoodoo), use divinatory tools and techniques, and invoke, summon, and even assume representations of their godhead; but a formal mechanism for conjuring spirits is omitted for some reason. Instead, witches employ magical energy techniques, such as the cone of power, to energize and add dynamism to their operations of thaumaturgy. This idea of using innate magical abilities and bodily based energies directed by one's will is a modern concept that would have been inconceivable a mere three centuries ago.

There are also informal mechanisms for contacting and engaging with spirits in Modern Witchcraft (such as local earth spirits or ancestors) but there doesn't appear to be a formal methodology. Witches in antiquity, as well as modern practitioners in the Afro-Caribbean traditions, use both an informal and a formal methodology. (A formal method is a deliberative summoning and an informal one is just making a connection. We will discuss this difference in greater detail later in this work.) I have often wondered about this strange fact, but then again I had to invent for myself a new methodology in order to develop the techniques of performing spirit conjurations.

As pointed out previously, the most important component in the ancient witchcraft regimen for spirit conjuring is the familiar spirit. Modern Witches are quite besotted with the concept of the animal familiar, as are many others in our modern world who love their various animal pets to the point of worship. However, a spirit familiar was not an animal pet, although it might assume the form of an animal. It could just as easily assume the form of a human. A spirit familiar was primarily a *spirit*, since it acted as the spiritual intermediary for the conjuring witch of antiquity. It also guarded or protected her (warded), and guided and taught her everything there was to know about spirits and the spirit world. The familiar spirit was an indispensable helper in the task of spirit conjuring as according to the beliefs of the previous age, such magic would have been impossible without its mediation. Let's examine the legends and even the history of magic to help us understand the nature of this mysterious entity.

Much can be said about the familiar spirit in legend and also in historical records. Emma Wilby has written a useful book entitled *Cunning Folk and Familiar Spirits,* and we can examine a few of the salient points that she makes about familiar spirits.[2] "Cunning folk" was the name given to those practitioners of witchcraft who did good deeds with the knowledge and powers they possessed. Conversely, a witch was someone who practiced witchcraft to do harm to others. Their familiars were also believed to be different, where the cunning man or woman would receive a fairy as their spirit guide or familiar spirit, and a witch would possess a demon as her familiar. In actual practice, however, the cunning folk were adjudged ambivalently by their neighbors—a person who could heal or do good using magic could also afflict and do harm depending on their intentions. A cunning man or woman could just as easily be accused of being a witch, and there were in fact such individuals who had performed good magic but were persecuted as evil witches by the authorities.

"In early modern Britain both the cunning folk and witches claimed to perform with the help of familiar spirits, but it is

---

2   Emma Wilby, *Cunning Folk and Familiar Spirits: Shamanistic Visionary Traditions in Early Modern British Witchcraft and Magic* (Portland, OR: Sussex Academic Press, 2005), 53–54.

a witch's demon familiar, whether in the form of a man or an animal, which is most recognizable to people today." [3]

Fairy or demon, the entity called a familiar spirit was a creature of the spirit world, and it had the ability to reside and affect things in both the material and spiritual underworld. As a being, it was indeed a very specialized entity also very closely associated with the conjuror, since it possessed its wielder when active. A number of various chthonic deities and demigods in antiquity such as Hecate, Hermes, and Persephone, supposedly bestowed their supplicants with spirit helpers. Yet these spirits, like all spirits, were called *daimones* by the Greeks, which later Christian theologians interpreted as demons.

The Greeks believed that the spiritual intermediaries between the gods and mankind were neutral, solely the attribute of whatever deity under whose directive they acted. It would follow that the special spiritual intermediary between a conjuring witch and the spirit world was a specialized entity that would have been considered a daimon. The Neoplatonist philosopher Plotinus believed that each person has their own daimon. [4]

According to the body of spells and magic from the Greco-Egyptian world, called the Greek Magical Papyri or PGM, the specialized familiar spirit was called a *parhedros* or magical servant (from Greek *para* and *hedros*—"near" or "close to one's side"). [5] The first two hundred lines of that text deal with spells that help the magician obtain a magical servant. So it would seem that in such a large body of collected magical lore, the most important first step for a magician would be acquiring one.

---

3   *Cunning Folk*, 46.

4   Bengt Ankarloo and Stewart Clark, eds., *Witchcraft and Magic in Europe: Ancient Greece and Rome* (London: The Athlone Press, 1999), 285.

5   Stephen Skinner, *Techniques of Graeco-Egyptian Magic* (St. Paul, MN: Llewellyn Publications, 2014), 288.

In Anna Scibilia's article entitled "Supernatural Assistant in the Greek Magical Papyri," she demonstrated that the authors of the various spells of the PGM had different opinions about the nature of this spirit and the methods for acquiring one.[6] The overall objective was the transformation of the practitioner through the execution of specific rites so that he or she would be able to participate in the sphere of the gods. This was done by either procuring a parhedros or divine assistant or through a process called *syntasis*, where the magician presented himself to the deity in a form of binding personal service. While the parhedros was believed to be an individual supernatural assistant separate from the magician, it could also appear in many different forms depending on the context of the magical spell. The parhedros could assume a human shape and in some cases was also called the holy guardian angel. In other instances the parhedros could be identified directly with a personalized deity, and still in other situations it could be associated with a specific magical object such as an inscribed tablet. It appears that there was no single unified perspective or opinion regarding this entity; many opinions were held simultaneously, some of them even contradictory.

One of the points Ms. Scibilia makes in her article is very close to what I am proposing in this book, that the magician performs rites and practices that allow identification with a specific deity to the degree of producing a kind of godhead identity. The parhedros is considered nothing more than a physical manifestation of that powerful and internal relationship.

> *"The operator regularly identifies himself with the divinity. He tries to take possession of the god's true name with the purpose of approaching a superior power that will guarantee his ability to act*

6   Jan N. Bremmer and Jan R. Veenstra, eds., *The Metamorphosis of Magic* (Dudley, MA: Peeters, 2002), 75–76.

in an inner-worldly context by means of knowledge originating from a communio with the divinity.”[7]

Returning to the biblical legend of the Witch of En-dor, she was called in Hebrew a *baal ab*, or mistress of a divining or familiar spirit. According to Morton Smith, an *ob* (pronounced "ov") is a spirit of the dead or minor underworld deity that "speaks from the earth in whispering voices."[8]

They are also objects of worship whose spirit can enter into a human and reside within them. Thus one who possesses a familiar spirit is also one who is possessed by it. This explanation might seem illogical until one examines the equivalent helper spirit that shamans employed since earliest times.

The Old Testament book of Samuel 1, chapter 28, verses 7 through 25, tells us the story about Saul consulting the Witch of En-dor.

Then Saul said to his servants, "Find a woman who is a necromancer for me to go and consult her." His servants replied, "There is a necromancer at En-dor."[9]

A necromancer was someone who could raise and communicate with the ghosts of the dead. It was another name for a conjuring witch who had the ability to enter into the spirit world, talk with the spirits of the dead, and relate their words (to a paying client) as prophecy. Saul visits the witch and asks her to perform magic for him. Although he was disguised, she apparently saw through it.

---

7 *Metamorphosis of Magic*, 73–74.

8 Morton Smith, *Jesus the Magician* (New York: Harper and Row, 1978), 77–78.

9 Alexander Jones, ed., *The Jerusalem Bible: Reader's Edition* (Garden City, NY: Doubleday and Co, 1968), 325.

Disclose the future to me." He [Saul] said, "by means of a ghost
[ob]. Conjure up the one I shall name for you."

Of course, the witch demands that she be held be immune from any recriminations or legal entanglements (witchcraft was illegal, of course). Saul swears this on the life of Yahweh, and that seems to settle the matter.

Then the woman asked, "Whom shall I conjure up for you?" He
replied, "Conjure up Samuel."

Of course, the witch now knows without a doubt that her potential client is King Saul and she feigns fear at this revelation, but Saul directs her to the task of conjuring the ghost of Samuel. He asks her to tell him what she sees, and she replies.

"I see a ghost rising up from the earth." "What is he like?" he asked.
She answered, "It is an old man coming up; he is wrapped in a cloak."

Of course we all know how the story ends, that the ghost of Samuel comes before Saul and prophesizes his death in the upcoming battle with the Philistines. There is no doubt that the witch has accomplished her objective, and what is communicated to Saul through the power of her familiar spirit is indisputably authentic.

Meeting a familiar spirit, according to Wilby, occurred spontaneously and unexpectedly to the witch or cunning person.[10] It typically happened when subjects were preoccupied by some catastrophic life-changes that were pushing them to their own extinction. Acquiring a spirit familiar could occur through a gift from another practitioner

---

10   *Cunning Folk*, 60.

(usually a family member). It could also be a gift from the King or Queen of the Fairies if the proto-witch happened to encounter one of them and kneeled before them in homage. However, the familiar, once acquired, would offer help and supernatural assistance to the budding witch, promising to teach her all of the secrets and arcane ways of the spirit world. Such help often quickly changed the fortunes of the witch for the better, since she now had a new and much more powerful vocation as a wielder of magic. Sometimes this agreement was established with a pact or binding agreement, but the relationship was considered a lifelong commitment, since it only ended with torture and death of the witch. Additionally, a witch or cunning person might have more than one familiar to aid them in their work.

According to Mircea Eliade's book *Shamanism*, the proto-shaman encountered his "tutelary" spirit when gravely ill.[11] In Siberia, a shaman ordinarily doesn't pick a spirit guide, called an *ayami*—he is instead chosen by it. In a weakened state, the shaman is hardly able to resist the intrusive spirit guide, but often tries to resist and fails. Typically, the spirit guide is part of a constellation of spirits who are also part of the family tree of shamans. Thus they can also be seen as ancestor spirits who operate within the shaman's family tribe. They can also be seen as a celestial bride that the shaman marries and keeps separately in a spiritual household. Once bound to the shaman, an ayami can offer other spirit servants, called *syven*, but they are subject to the will and power of the spirit guide and represent the constellation of spirits who reside and interact with the shaman, all within the sphere of the shaman's magical domain—the conscious mind.

It would seem to me that the various lore about the shaman spirit guide, the familiar spirit of the witch or cunning person, the parhedros

---

11   Mircea Eliade, *Shamanism: Archaic Techniques of Ecstasy* (Princeton, NJ: Princeton University Press, 1992), 71–76.

of Greco-Egyptian magic, the ob or ghost helper of the witch of Endor are all essentially depicting the same kind of entity. Since there are plenty of examples of how a person in antiquity could actively acquire a familiar spirit, we can also conclude that the shamanic ayami was an entity that could be sought by the shaman as well as accidently encountered. The spiritual intermediary appears to have an ancient pedigree that extends into the distant and unknowable past. As a traditional component for spirit conjuring it is still relevant today, although its form has been modified somewhat.

A familiar spirit as the witch's assistant has certainly undergone some changes over time, just as many other components of magic and culture have changed as well. Some of the qualities of the familiar spirit were that it was a spirit that could assume many forms and perform many functions; it acted like a mediator between the spirit world and the material world. A familiar spirit could also function as the guardian, guide, and soul-extension of the witch. Of course, there were exceptions and even contradictions that would not propose a seamless and single definition.

In some cases it seemed that a familiar spirit was possessed by the witch and also possessed the witch as well. In this case it would appear that once acquired that the familiar spirit was wholly identified with the witch, thereby functioning as an external spiritual entity that could be projected by her into the spirit or material world. It would also seem that the familiar spirit was some kind of functioning over-soul for the witch, and it was an integral part of her being. Paradoxically, it was both within her and without her; both a separate and distinct entity and an appendage of her spiritual body. This kind of being has entered into the modern world as something besides a separate and distinct spiritual being. However, this was not always the case, and often as not the familiar spirit was just a servant for the witch, and it could be one of many such servants.

Some additional modern definitions of the familiar spirit might consist of the terms "alter ego," "spirit control," "extended self," "external soul," and even "doppelganger." The question is whether this intimate spirit guide or familiar could also be equated with the higher attributes of the self, such as the holy guardian angel, genius, or augoeides. I believe that these terms are similar because of the fact that the familiar spirit was such an intimate part of the conjuring witch, and it also functioned as a higher self-extension that could bridge the gap or gateway between the worlds. Of course there were exceptions, and not everyone today would agree that these distinctly different entities could be lumped together to satisfy one specific definition. In fact there are quite a spectrum of opinions about whether or not these various entities can be considered variations of one single concept today, as I have found out when I happened to ask my Wiccan, Pagan, and magical peer group about it.

Still, in my opinion, and due to the affect that more than two millennia of Christianity has had on the consciousness of Western culture, the effects of transcendentalism have greatly changed the definition of the spirit guide, elevating it to a much higher level. Based on my operational hypothesis, the spirit guide has become the active expression of the self as godhead, since it now can be identified with the Hindu concept of *atman*, or god/dess-within, a feature of Modern Witchcraft and Paganism. I believe we can somewhat redefine the attributes of the familiar spirit in order for it to have a meaningful context in the practice of modern Witchcraft; just as money from a past epoch would need to be converted in order for modern people to understand the monetary power and standard of living of the people at that time. Still, I had stated that Plotinus believed that human beings possessed a daimon or spiritual intermediary between themselves and the deities, so perhaps this revision is in keeping with the Neoplatonism of the previous age of antiquity. It certainly was somewhat in agreement with the spells and practices used by the sorcerers who compiled the PGM. If we consider that such a spirit would act as the emissary of some deity then it might also be construed that each person is bound to a specific godhead—their own personalized deity.

Therefore, if I am saying that the familiar spirit is the activated and internalized Godhead residing in a person then what is the nature of the kind of magic that a modern conjuring witch would perform using this as her basic premise? A conjuring witch, both in the previous age and in modern times would use a system of magic that I would call the spirit theory or model of magic. Some have strongly promoted that the practice of modern magic should be a spirit-only methodology, but that is too limiting, in my opinion. I define the spirit theory of magic as a system or methodology that causes magical effects and phenomena through the conjuration and manipulation of various types and qualities of spirits. It includes first and foremost the possession and wielding of a familiar spirit to facilitate access to the domain of spirit. Even so, what I am proposing would represent a kind of magic where the practitioner would function as both a human agency and also as a deity.

A spirit theory of magic would also propose that we live in a world that is the intersection of two domains, which are the material and spiritual worlds. It would also propose that the spirit world, being a simulacrum of our own world, would consist of three interacting locations (spheres), which are the heavens, the earth, and the underworld. Each of these worlds are populated with many spirits, consisting of deities; demigods and lesser gods; mythical creatures and people; ancestral ghosts; angels and demons; astrological, planetary, and elemental spirits; fairies and earth spirits; and a host of other entities of location and place too numerous to list. The spirit world occupies the same space as the material world, yet only fully conscious beings with material bodies can exist in both. This division of the world is replicated in shamanism and in every primitive culture known to anthropologists. Despite the differences of sophistication and technology, it appears that modern magical perspectives and their ancient antecedents are in agreement.

The simple way to demarcate the spirit world as distinguished from the material world would be to draw a circular boundary. Unlike the Ceremonial Magical circle, this kind of circle would represent the simple boundary between the sacred and profane worlds. It would not function as a protective ring; that is how the circle is used in Ceremonial Magic. The use of this boundary in some form was a standard trope in antiquity, representing the threshold between the normal world and sacred precincts of a temple or grove. Since Modern Witches use a magic circle in the same manner as the ancient polytheists did, this is a natural component of any magical or liturgical working. Other symbolic structures could be employed as well, such as the triangle gateway, but the circle is the first and most important component of such a working, particularly if there is no building or structure to represent such a boundary.

Additionally, a spirit theory of magic would also propose the distinction between summoning one's familiar spirit, calling a deity or summoning an external spirit, whether beneficial, neutral, or potentially hostile. In common parlance a sorcerer performing a conjuration would *invoke* a deity, a beneficial spirit (such as an angel), and would *evoke* a spirit that is neutral or hostile. "Invocation" comes from the Latin *invocare*, meaning to call a spirit into one's self or summon down from above. "Evocation" comes from the Latin *evocare*, meaning to call a spirit from outside or below oneself. One therefore invokes a beneficial spirit from the location of the heavens (including one's familiar spirit) and evokes a neutral or hostile spirit from the location of the earth or underworld. On the surface, this rule is much too simple and there are a number of notable exceptions. We will go over this concept in more detail in a later chapter.

Magical operations used to conjure a spirit can be quite involved and appear complicated, but they are actually rather simple, consisting as they do of five steps or stages. These steps are performed in some manner whether explicitly or implicitly. The more mature and evolved the conjuring witch, the more automatic and internalized the stages will be performed. The Witch of En-dor seemed to engage in little preparation work and was able to achieve a successful manifestation within a short period of time. Typically, a conjuring witch will take more time than the biblical story would seem to demonstrate. Neutral or hostile spirits would require more time for preparation and would need constraining and binding.

The five steps of a formal method for spirit conjuration are given as *preparation, summoning, constraining, binding,* and then *releasing.* Preparation for a working would require a period of time for the conjuring witch to focus, visualize, sacralize the place of conjuration, and then prepare for the actual conjuration. The summoning occurs at the appointed predetermined time within the sanctified sacred space established through purifications and sacramental offerings, and then a circular boundary is drawn. I have determined through extensive research that the method for summoning or calling a spirit is exactly the inverse of an exorcism; even the language used is similar. I was able to determine this by comparing the pre-Vatican II Catholic rite of exorcism with the more classical evocations found in old grimoires.

Constraining and binding were techniques typically reserved for neutral or hostile spirits. I would define hostile spirits as entities that are angry and uncooperative, and this could include some demons, earth spirits as well as uncooperative ancestor spirits. When the Witch of En-dor summoned the reluctant ghost of Samuel, you can well imagine that she would have constrained and bound him for the duration of the operation. These operations can be performed in a number of different ways, and one can see in the phraseology used the alliterations to the art of ligature. If a consecrated cord was used in a spirit conjuring (as it probably was in antiquity), the tying and tightening of the knots would be the constraining and binding of a spirit trapped within the core of the knot, while releasing of the spirit would be simply untying the knots and freeing it. Early forms of Traditional and Modern Witchcraft used knots in this fashion for cord magic although not to specifically bind, constrain, and release spirits.

Other methods for capturing and binding spirits were through the use of pots of water or earth, iron chains and also brass containers. Spirits could be bound and sealed in a brass bottle, much like the brass lamp containing a powerful djinni in the *Arabian Nights*. Constraining was focusing and receiving the spirit after it appeared, and binding was applying it to a specific task or purpose. It could also involve an agreement, pact, or offering. Releasing was nothing more than giving the spirit permission to depart.[12] The differences in how conjurors conducted themselves with the spirit often indicated whether their attitudes toward the evoked spirit were of domination or mutual respect. Later grimoires treated potentially hostile spirits (like demons) in a highly coercive and dominating manner due to the theological opinions about them found within Christianity and Judaism.

One of the most important components for conjuration was the mark, signature, seal, character, or sigil that identified the spirit. The spirit's name was also very important, too. Having the name of the spirit could at least give the conjure witch a mechanism for producing a character or mark identifying that spirit. Such an identifying mark could be carved or engraved on a metal, ceramic, or beeswax tablet or drawn with ink on a shard of pottery or a piece of cloth, animal skin, papyrus, or parchment. Not knowing the name or the mark of a spirit would certainly cause any conjuration to fail, so this information was vital to a successful operation.[13] It was important to be able to identify the spirit thoroughly before the summoning was performed. In some cases,

---

12   Stephen Skinner and David Rankine, *The Goetia of Dr. Rudd* (Woodbury, MN: Llewellyn Publications, 2010), 65–66.

13   A name can also be substituted for an attribute or other qualifier. A fairy could have a name like *Brown Tom* or *Thistle Top*, or a home spirit, *Door Guardian*.

spirits that are very familiar to the conjuror, such as spirits of the home and hearth, might not actually have names but would instead have attributes and associations.

Knowing the name, mark, and the associative hierarchy of the spirit as well as any other attributes such as those found in various occult correspondences like colors, perfumes, incense, planetary and elemental qualities, gem stones, metals, minerals, plants and herbs, mythic images, or mystical signs would therefore greatly assist the conjuring process. The more knowledge that the conjuror possessed about the spirit greatly increased the impact of the conjuration, ensuring a successful outcome and making it more powerful and meaningful.

Sacrifices, such as bloody animal sacrifices, were an important part of certain kinds of conjuration exercises usually having to do with underworld spirits; they are not necessary in our modern age. I believe there are many substitutions for an actual animal sacrifice, but it was likely that this was a historical feature in many operations where spirits were summoned. Considering the fact that institutionalized animal sacrifices occurred on a regular basis in the state-sanctioned cults of the ancient world and that the cooked meat from such sacrifices represented the only times that the poorer folk got to eat meat in any quantity, private sacrifices would also have been a normal occurrence for the wealthy. Such offerings for a goetic rite would have been made to the chthonic deities as well as to the spirits being summoned. Food and drink would also have been given as offerings, as would flowers, incense, perfumes, and votive lights or fires.

Sacred space, specialized vestments, and the proper location and time would also have been factors in conjuration. If she lived in a specific locality, a conjuring witch might perform spirit summoning in her home, but conjurations could also be performed near temple precincts (or within a temple if it would grant such authorization), graveyards, recent battlefields, ruined buildings, swamps, caves, or near bodies of water that were tainted by underground noxious emissions. Itinerant performers would likely choose a neglected or deserted area for maximum privacy. The timing would depend on whether any additional auspices were used such as planning the working at night during an auspicious astronomical event, just after dusk or before dawn (twilight gateways), or at some other special time. The moon could be waxing or waning, and other astronomical or astrological portends could be consulted and used.

When all of these components for a specific conjuration were brought together by an experienced conjuror (usually for a paying client), the resultant operation was certain to produce some amazing results. The client was certainly on edge from all of the preparations and the spooky atmosphere and embellishments, to say nothing of the conjuror's crooning, moaning, and shrieking evocative cries in some barbarous, unknown tongue. It undoubtedly produced a powerful effect one would not soon forget. Even if the client was stone cold sober (which was not very likely), the experience would have been horrific— but it would have produced the expected results.

From the perspective of the Modern Witch or Pagan, many of these ritual components and magical elements are still very relevant today; other practices can be substituted with more acceptable and modern techniques. Yet despite the fact that some of these techniques would have to be redefined and translated into a more modern magical technology, the Modern Witch and Pagan still have the basic structures and methodologies imbedded in their own tradition to practice the formalized art of conjuration safely and without any fear of spiritual possession, obsession, or psychological trauma. What is required are some additional components added to the basic repertoire of the Witch and the Pagan who are practicing both magic and liturgy within their sacred space.

What this means is that Modern Witches and Pagans can perform the high art of conjuration within the boundaries of their own traditions without having to either adopt the Golden Dawn magical tradition or the grimoire system of ceremonial magic. They can do these kinds of workings without any worries or hazards, safely and effectively. I can verify that this is a fact because I myself have been doing this kind of magic over the last thirty or more years without having any kind of negative consequences or pathological breakdowns. I don't believe that what I discovered years ago was so personal and idiosyncratic that it can't be shown and shared to any who want to perform this kind of magic.

I have successfully taught many others to perform this kind of magic, and I am confident that I can teach you to do it as well. You will need only the most basic tools and supplies, some of which you probably already have. You won't have to purchase expensive and exotic tools, materials, or read and study a lot of obscure or obtuse books on the subject. It is my objective to show you how everything can be done efficiently and effectively. I will also show you how to develop a magical discipline for spirit conjuration. I can even help you select some of the old grimoires so you can appropriate various lore, sigils, seals, characters, and talismans from them if you want to learn more about the subject.

So now that we have set the stage by defining what the legendary witches did in order to conjure spirits and have established our objectives for building up an extended magical discipline, we can move on to the next phase of this work and get down to the practical application of spirit conjuration.

Modern Witchcraft and Repurposing of Spirit Conjuration

Stars hide your fires! Let not light see
my black and deep desires.
MACBETH, SCENE IV

One of my friends in the craft once told me that Modern Witches do indeed interact and work with spirits, and that an elaborate approach to doing this wasn't really needed. What he said surprised me a bit—actually, it stung, since I have been something of a zealot in promoting a formal approach to spirit conjuring and making it a major part of Modern Witchcraft. What could he mean? Were my efforts in this direction based on confusion? Was I just out of touch with what other Witches did?

After thinking about what he said for a while and talking to others, I came to the conclusion that what he was really talking about was an informal engagement with spirits instead of a formal and deliberate conjuration. There is a big difference between encountering and engaging spirits and formally focusing on one specific spirit and summoning it to appear. This realization also forced me to think about the dynamics of Modern Witchcraft and to realize objectively that Witchcraft practitioners could quite easily engage with spirits informally because they did their work at the periphery of the spirit world.

The key to my dilemma is the consecrated magic circle that Witches habitually use as well as the realization that it is a true boundary between the material and spirit worlds. If properly set and consecrated (and I mean if those in the circle visualize it as such), the magic circle of the Witches would place them at the very threshold of the worlds of mankind and the world of spirits. In such an environment, anyone could easily encounter spirits either familiar to one (such as earth spirits of place and location) or intimate (such as genetic or spiritual ancestor spirits). Without formally calling and naming, constraining and binding them, there could be a veritable ocean of spirits around a magic circle, and the operators within it might be aware of only a small subset. Formally calling and naming them gives them a concrete objectivity they might not ordinarily have. It also establishes a powerful relationship and gives them a singular purpose and function. Individuals who are regularly exposed to the spiritual influences of the magic circle can, over time, sense and informally engage with spirits without actually being in a circle.

Additionally, the magic circle is a protected interstice between the worlds that is guarded by the Goddess and God of the covenstead tradition. They are always summoned and called in some manner or sometimes even assumed by the priestess or priest, so they are the active deities that ensure that everything that occurs in the magic circle is positive and safe. Like overprotective parents, these deities could also make certain that the coven members don't engage with troublesome neutral or hostile spirits. They would also make certain that the coven members don't call or summon something that might endanger them and their followers. Therefore, they keep a watchful eye out for their "children" and don't allow them to wander off into the spirit world, make mischief, or get into trouble. This analogy is probably overly simplistic, but it does convey the idea that Witches do their work in a protected and insulated threshold domain. They don't typically attempt to explore that world more deeply or engage with entities that could be troublesome. There are inherent prohibitions or taboos against performing deliberate conjurations of neutral or hostile spirits in a coven-based circle, even though they are usually unstated. The dread lords who protect the four Watchtowers also ensure that the sacred space of a magic circle is safe and durable from both the outside and the inside.

It is my opinion that the Witch's magic circle is an open gateway to the entire spirit world. The only thing that stands between a rather scary encounter with a hostile or callous neutral spirit is the ever-present guardianship of the Goddess and God and the belief invested in them by the coven. They make the magic circle a safe place to gather while the Watchtowers act as beacons that keep out profane and unwanted external influences. Bear in mind that I am talking about Modern Witches who are properly trained and experienced—beginners get to experience more meaningful and profound encounters with the deities and the wards of the cardinal directions over time. When such an encounter hits a tipping point then the beginner often experiences some trauma, necessitating an assisted grounding afterward; but even these encounters are considered benign since they are associated with friendly and helpful deities and spirits. How much more harsh and difficult would such an encounter be if the beginner somehow encountered a neutral or hostile spirit?

It is for this reason that a formal conjuration of spirits is not part of the typical regimen of the Modern Witch, and why the traditional Book of Shadows doesn't contain this kind of rite within its pages. One could assume that Modern Witches have developed a methodology that makes their liturgy and magic both safe and effective. While I believe that such insulation from the greater spirit world is probably a good thing for beginners and inexperienced individuals, it can also hamper more potent and transformative magical practices. At some point in time it becomes important to grow up and move beyond the confining scrutiny of the deities and the Watchtowers and delve deeper into the spirit world and thereby experience the domain of spirits in all its glory, mystery, and (at times) even fearful terror. If we are kept in a safe habitat, we will never realize the true challenges and the corresponding empowerment associated with independent action and discovery. Yet the real question is how to do this without imperiling oneself.

Another important consideration is that Witches need a reason to move beyond the protective veil of their coven-based traditions to encounter the whole spectrum and geography of the Spirit World. As was put to me by my friend, why would anyone want to summon a spirit that might cause harm, maliciously or unwittingly? Why summon a hostile spirit or a demon, angel, or anything else outside the provenance of the covenstead, the warding deities, or friendly spirits? Why bother when one apparently has everything needed to work magic or liturgical rites?

I can more easily answer this question by putting it in a different and humorous way: Why move away from your parents' home when they have supported and taken care of you for so many years? The reason is that we are expected to grow, evolve, and become independent both materially and spiritually. Likewise, we deal with different people in our normal lives and careers, some of whom are hot-headed or passionate (hostile), some who are callous or indifferent (neutral), and others who are intimate friends; these can be family, spouses, allies, workmates, business partners, bosses, subordinates, worthy opponents, enemies, lifelong friends, and even lovers. We have to deal with all kinds of people in order to function in the world, even sometimes people who are unpleasant or potentially hostile. So, too, we need to deal with many different spirits to learn all we can from the spiritual world in order to master it.

The best way to cope with a complex material life is to be cautious about passing judgments on individuals and groups and engage everyone and anything that happens with an open mind. The same attitude is also important when approaching the spirit world. To make prejudicial judgments about fairies, demons, angels, ghosts, or any other kind of spirit is to handicap the ability to learn, evolve, and expand while engaging with that world. My assumption is that Witches are not part of the Abrahamic family of religions. We are not "people of the book" and have no holy scriptures. Our holy book is based completely on our experiences with the gods, nature, the inherent mysteries of life, the world of spirit, and the transcendental power of magic.

Though we are the recipients of a cultural legacy of beliefs, myths, and practices, we do not need to take upon ourselves the same opinions and attitudes toward the spirit world that others who are Christian might possess. Instead, we should approach all spirits with an open mind. We should make judgments based purely upon our own experience instead of passively adopting culturally programmed associations. I believe any Modern Witch should treat all spirits with respect and a certain amount of reverence since they are the intermediaries between the gods and humanity regardless of their overall class or place in the spiritual geography. Approaching spirits as some kind of hostile, threatening, and inimical "other" as some of the old grimoires suggest is exactly the wrong mindset to use when approaching the formal rites of invocation and evocation.

What this means is that we should suspend our innate prejudice and culturally determined opinions that would make us judge demons as uniformly evil, angels as uniformly good, and fairies as cute, sweet, and ineffectual entities. All of these cultural opinions and beliefs need to be discarded as an interfering cultural bias residing within a massive collection of misinformation. *Whatever we experience when encountering spirits will become the subjective facts we will use to build up our own foundation of knowledge.* Nothing can be taken for granted and nothing can be assumed. If a would-be conjuror can learn to be open minded and disregard what is supposedly common knowledge about these spirits, then he or she will be able to do this work in a more productive manner and also without fear or prejudice. I can also factually state that how we approach these spirits will be mirrored in how they interact with whomever summons them.

These statements that I am making about spirits and our cultural disposition toward them are the most important ones that a would-be conjuring Witch or Pagan should thoughtfully consider and take to heart before ever attempting to perform an invocation or evocation. I want the student to start out on the right foot, as it were, and avoid erroneous assumptions and cultural opinions wherever possible. This should be the most important step a student takes when beginning to learn the art of spirit conjuration. It requires some critical thinking on the part of a serious student to consider that all beliefs and attitudes about spirits should be based upon real experiences; where such knowledge is lacking, the student is advised to suspend judgment until he or she knows from experience. Therefore, the real classification of spirits is built up through a process of experiential knowledge with the caveat that all spirits are unique, different, individualistic, and don't conform to stereotypes unless the conjuror insists they do. The spirit world is very mutable because it resides wholly within the domain of consciousness and it has little if any actual physical basis in our objective reality. This means that our attitudes, opinions, beliefs, and our feelings will impact what we see, hear, and sense when engaged with that world.

A student conjuror is a person who has some experience already in their chosen tradition of Witchcraft and Paganism. This kind of operation is not really for absolute beginners. Everyone has to start somewhere on the path of Witchcraft or Paganism, but performing conjurations is particularly the skillset of the intermediate student at the very least. In the repurposing of the magic employed in Witchcraft, the student has mastered the basic skills associated with their religious and magical tradition. Spirit conjuration is a very strict discipline, but it is not something that is difficult to attain or too obscure to understand. The task is to present the relevant skills that a student conjuror needs to possess and that he or she has already obtained from following a specific tradition be it from hands-on training through coven teachers, one on one from a mentor, in the fellowship with other students, or as a solitary student making use of books and other materials. If the student has learned to become competent in the specific skills to be employed in conjuring, he or she will be able to acquire and fully deploy the techniques outlined in this book.

We have already covered the remarkable qualities of the Witches' consecrated magic circle and established that it creates a boundary between the sacred and profane worlds, opening up those who wield it to the spirit world. Various traditions have different ways of building and generating sacred space, some are more elaborate than others. There are also variances depending on where this sacred space is to be located. A temporary room used in the home has different requirements than a permanent temple or an outdoor grove. Typically, a grove requires very little in terms of "making" sacred space since it is assumed to be sacred at all times. A grove does have some kind of boundary, and crossing it triggers the same process as when an indoor space is being consecrated and warded. Establishing and generating sacred space in some form is a critically important step in the techniques of conjuring since it defines the gateway between worlds.

At some point a student will have to learn and adopt the methodologies of controlling consciousness. The foundation for this practice is meditation, and the key to meditation is where the subject focuses on his or her breathing. Breath control, such as internally counting during the phases of inhalation, holding in the breath, exhalation, and then holding the breath while the lungs are empty is the basic cyclic method for establishing a powerful meditative state. Meditation can be basically divided into four technics or yogas: developing a solid sitting posture (asana), breath-control (prana-yama), intoning words (mantra), and staring at a fixed point or diagram (yantra).

Additionally, the student can attempt to empty the mind of all thoughts or to focus on only one thing for a short period (contemplation), focusing on a single idea or concept while excluding all other thoughts (concentration) or enter into a shallow or deep self-induced hypnotic trance. The basic mindset used in these exercises is one that is called mindfulness, in that whatever happens the subject remains in a state of openness, receptivity that is nonjudgmental. These practices should be familiar in some form or another and should be practiced on a regular basis or at least until they become automatic.

The mind-state fostered by meditation is the foundation for all magical work, particularly any magical work that requires a deeper awareness than what might be typically performed by a group in a coven. Trance is also an important mind-state since it is the mechanism through which one can assume a godhead, also known to Witches and Pagans as a drawing down of the sun, moon, or some other deity. Whether the student has spent any time in learning and experiencing a godhead assumption or if it is something that she has either read about or just witnessed as a coven member is unimportant. Part of the exercises for learning to conjure spirits will require her to not only learn and experience this technique but to master it through repetitious and continual practice.

As I have pointed out that the Goddess and God of a tradition or coven (or one's own developed tradition) are the guardians of the magic circle and the protectors of the group who performs their rites, so do these deities help make the experience of Witchcraft safe and effective. Anyone who wants to progress beyond the sanctuary of this comfortable situation must assume a personal godhead that will function as a guide and protector before embarking on a working that will extend the magic circle into the full domain of spirits. This godhead assumption is similar to the famous spirit familiar of the previous ages; adopting a continuous regimen to assume that personal aspect of deity is to develop a spiritual extension of one's being that represents one as a God or Goddess.

In a magical context the Witch is no longer alone in the extended magic circle but is covered and masked by the power and authority of her personal godhead. There can be no greater protection, guidance, or empowerment than the full assumption of a deity prior to performing any kind of spiritual conjuration. Therefore, the Witch trades in the Goddess and God of her Witchcraft coven and tradition for her own personal and assumed godhead in order to be fully protected and empowered within the spirit world.

Godhead assumption is a mechanism that is absolutely required for spirit conjuring if the Witch or Pagan is using a magic circle that exposes her to the domain of spirits instead of protecting her from the harm and contagion that might occur during an evocation. A Witch using a consecrated magic circle is completely vulnerable to the domain of spirits, particularly when the circle is fully opened and extended into that world. The various guardians and the deities of the covenstead can no longer protect her if that circle is extended.

How a magic circle is extended is through the simple use of a cross roads and a triangular structure within the circle that makes a gateway drawn by the Witch. We will talk more about that later, but there are a number of simple devices that allow Witches to perform workings of high magic without having to invest in either the Golden Dawn- or grimoire-based systems of magic.

While assuming a godhead is a requirement, this operation cannot be accomplished unless the Witch has first developed a personal relationship with that deity. The relationship between human and deity is called a spiritual alignment, and there are five basic components that work together to build up a suitable spiritual relationship between the deity and Witch. These categories apply to the practice of Witchcraft but could be modified to apply to any religious, magical discipline. The five categories are devotion, invocation, godhead assumption, communion, and spiritual service.

Devotion: This category consists of all of the practices and obligations that a Witch assumes in order to properly worship the gods. Votive offerings are a large part of this work, as are meditations, prayers, the reciting or singing of special hymns, paeans, poetic expressions, and the giving of signs of submission and dedication (bowing, kneeling, laying prone before the shrine, and so on). Votive offerings consist of lighting candles, burning incense, placing offerings of flowers arranged in a decorative bouquet, and they can—and should—include the offerings of food and drink. Sometimes the offerings are given to the earth, either poured or buried or to fire as burnt offerings. Some offerings are forms of sacrifice, where a precious object is given to the deity and used exclusively ever after in that shrine. We have already talked about the sacrifice of animals, but that is something that should only be attempted by individuals or groups who are experienced and knowledgeable in the proper ritual killing and butchering of animals. It is also necessary that sacrificial animals would also be used as food for human consumption, thus eliminating most creatures from any list. Most of us (including myself) should be able to adequately satisfy our deities with the typical offerings of light, incense, flowers, and food and drink—the very things we ourselves enjoy.

One important element that assists in the practice of spiritual and liturgical devotion is the preparation and use of some kind of shrine for the deities. Whether the room used for performing the work of Witchcraft is one that is temporary or permanent, there should be a place where a small table or wall niche holds the deities' symbolic representations.

This place can be covered up and obscured or prominently displayed, but it becomes the permanent focus in the household for all of the work of spiritual devotion either way. I call such a place a shrine, and if you don't have such a place then creating one is an important step in learning to master the art of spirit summoning.

Many Witches have some kind of shrine or even multiple places where religious artifacts are placed in their homes. It represents the idea that the deities live in that house and are the spiritual core of that domain. This is something that Witches, Pagans, and polytheists in other nations such as India or even ancient Egypt, Greece, or Rome share in common with each other. I consider having a shrine in one's home to be a very important component in the practice of higher forms of ritual magic. It is also important to develop a discipline to perform the various tasks of devotion in a daily, weekly, monthly, and seasonal periodicity. Making spiritual devotion a regular part of one's religious and magical discipline will also make performing the specialized tasks associated with summoning spirits a lot easier. Devotion to one's deities simply becomes extended to a form of devotion to all spirits.

Invocation: While devotion represents a kind of periodic spiritual maintenance, invocation is the formal mechanism where one deliberately calls and summons one or more of the deities. Typically, this is done after the consecration of sacred space and the setting of a magic circle. The four wards are called and the Watchtowers are established, and within that protected environment, the deities—usually in the form of a Goddess and a God—are called. Some groups may call or summon deities specifically by name (as determined by the tradition or covenstead), while some might call a generic Goddess and God. My opinion is that the deities summoned should be specifically named and the qualities and characteristics of that deity known by all in attendance. I feel that this is very important, and that individuals and groups shouldn't summon any deity (or spirit, for that matter) unless it has been named, defined, and fully characterized.

Godhead Assumption: We have already briefly covered this practice, but I wanted to add more details. Godhead assumption is a fancy and formal way of saying performing a draw, such as drawing down the sun, moon, or the Horned God. It is a form of trance-induced possession where the body and mind of the subject performing it becomes overlaid by the character and personality of the target deity. Performing this rite incorporates the practices of devotion, invocation, and consciousness control. Like most religion-based phenomena, being possessed by a god is something that the priestess or priest performs without completely surrendering their will or personal volition. They practice and prepare for this rite in a very serious and rigorous manner, and the resultant manifestation of deity that emanates from them varies in its quality depending on the abilities, timing, state of mind, preparation, and previous built-up experience they possess and bring to this operation.

In the reclaiming tradition of Witchcraft, godhead assumption is called "aspecting," and like similar practices in Afro-Caribbean religions such as Voudoun and Santería, where worshippers are ridden by the loa or orisha demigods, anyone can share in the experience of being possessed by a deity—not just the facilitator.[14] This is a more egalitarian approach to godhead assumption than what is typically practiced in British traditions of Witchcraft. It is something I am proposing should be a normal part of what the individual conjuring Witch would formally practice in

---

14   See the online magazine *Reclaiming Quarterly* for the article "Aspecting in the Reclaiming Tradition" by Sage at www.reclaimingquarterly.org/86/rq-86-aspectingreclaiming.html.

her magic. This term is now used outside the Reclaiming tradition to denote the transformation of someone (typically clergy) who emanates the presence of a deity.

Still, there is no greater realization of the mystery and majesty of the gods for Witches and Pagans than when such a godhead assumption is performed by an experienced and prepared priest or priestess acting within an established mythic and symbolic presentation. Such a presentation gives those attending a direct exposure and experience of the divine functioning in the sacralized world of a polytheistic faith. I have experienced this kind of presentation where it seemed that in the transfixed guise of the officiating priest or priestess, the god walked among the devoted worshippers and engaged with them directly.[15] I have also seen many examples where this kind of presentation was performed so badly that it seemed to be a petty insult to the deity as well as an object lesson in human gullibility. However, there are ways to ensure that such a working is both completely successful and entirely satisfying. I will discuss this in detail later in the book.

One of the most important rites in the art of spirit summoning is to learn to master the technique of godhead assumption so it becomes an automatic and internalized process. This rite is not just the provenance of priestesses and priests, since it is the method where the conjuring witch develops her personal deity into an internalized and powerful extension of her spiritual self. This will not only be an important topic for us to cover here, but it will be a necessary skill that anyone who seeks to formally summon spirits must master.

---

15 Perhaps the most notable of these Godhead draws is the revival of the Horned God drawing down mystery rite. In the Twin Cities of Minneapolis and St. Paul, this mystery rite has become something of an inner tradition celebrated at the Grand Sabbat every other year or two.

Communion: Where giving offerings to the deities typically represents a single direction of a devotee to godhead gift, communion is a form of reciprocity. Communion occurs when offerings, particularly food and drink, are given up to the deity as an offering. Once touched and blessed (thereby sacralizing them), they are given back to the devotees to share. Communion consists of making sacraments out of offerings and then dispensing them back to the devotees. How this occurs is through the agency of some kind of direct or indirect contact with the deity, whether that implies the offering is left in the shrine for a suitable period of time or it is directly blessed by the one acting as the deity through godhead assumption. In addition to food and drink, sacraments can also be other kinds of objects such as oils, perfumes, ointments, herbal caches, or any sacred object that can be imbued with the essence of the godhead. I should note that not all offerings become sacraments, since some quantity of the gifts to the deity must be kept and not relinquished so they can represent a kind of sacrifice or loss.

Spiritual Service: One of the least understood or practiced forms of spiritual alignment is spiritual service. If you receive the blessings of the deity for offerings and devotions, it is important to also pass them on to the community at large. Simply practicing a spiritual alignment between devotee and deity in an insular and socially closed manner doesn't allow for that relationship to be objectified in any manner. If we receive and are blessed by the gods, then we must also give back to the community in some form of spiritual service so the deity's presence is truly realized by many people, including outsiders. A closed coven that doesn't perform any kind of community work is one that has short-circuited its ability to truly realize the spiritual blessings of the Gods in the greater community. Even if that spiritual service is done in complete discretion and is unacknowledged, it will still count as spiritual service and allow for the fulfillment of the cycle of the manifestation of the blessings and emanation of the Gods. It also helps such a person retain their humanity and place in the world, and this is a critical counter point that a Witch needs to maintain in order to function in the real world while actively engaging with the spirit world. Spiritual service also represents all of the minor tasks associated with maintaining and serving the gods within a shrine.

One other element that is an important part of interacting with the gods is to perform divination on a regular basis. While a Witch or Pagan will typically use their runes or tarot cards to perform readings for critical life events or determining the future when times are insecure, I feel that a regular regimen of divination is important. As one performs daily meditations, it is also important to perform divination as well. Stated quite simply, divination is talking to the gods.

Since a conjuring Witch is engaged with expanding and extending her alignment with the deities, she must also converse with them on a regular basis. Some are gifted with the ability to actually mentally talk to the gods while praying or meditating and even receive mental replies, but many do not have this ability and so must employ divination to know what the gods know. I would recommend that the erstwhile conjuring Witch employ more direct methods of divination, such as dice or knucklebones, coins, pendulum, a magic mirror, crystal ball, or anything else that he or she can quickly use. Coins and dice are good for yes/no type questions, and this is often all that is needed for a quick answer. Cards, runes, or other tools require one to learn and practice in order to master them.

Something to remember is that when asking a question of the gods, one should ask it using a clear and concise question to a specific named deity, particularly one with whom the querent has already established an alignment. Then upon receiving the answer (whatever that answer might be) one should be thankful and not repeat the question again until much later. If you persist in asking the same question over and over again, you will undoubtedly earn the ironic rebuke and exasperated annoyance that often accompanies such disrespectful actions. Such repetitions produced skewed results, such as when a parent is badgered by child for the answer they want. The answer is usually no even when it might have been a yes or a maybe.

Astrology is also an important tool as it is the only divination system that can inform the conjuring Witch about any given planned operation's timeliness. While it isn't necessary for a Witch to be an adept astrologer, it does help to know something about her natal chart, the transits that might impact that natal chart, and also the times or phases of the moon and the sun. Because the lunar cycles and solar seasons affect the typical Witch's or Pagan's religious calendar, knowing something about the astronomy and astrology of these celestial orbs is important. The most important cycle for the practice of conjuration is the eight phases of the lunation cycle, which we will cover later in this work.

This brings us to the final consideration, and that is how to establish and build a spiritual and magical discipline. A discipline is nothing more than a series of practices and rites that are performed at certain times. Some of them are necessarily periodic and others are special events, such as performing a specific spirit summoning. The cycle of light and darkness is the ordering factor for a Witch or Pagan. This represents the mysteries of the cycle of day and night as well as the lunar and solar cycles of the month and year. The cycle of lunar months and the wheel of the year are already a part of the liturgical calendar of the practicing Witch and Pagan. The lunar cycle represents the passage of forces and powers that are decidedly hidden and within the domain of the unconscious mind. They also determine, along with the seasons, the time for planting and harvesting. So too does the lunar cycle stand as a mechanism for determining the best times for working certain kinds of magic.

While the kind and type of spirit has some bearing on the lunar cycle used to perform a conjuration, it is normal for magical work of this type to be started after the new moon and to be brought to fullness just before the moon becomes full. The waxing of the moon also affects the waxing of psychic and spiritual powers, while the waning moon represents a time of releasing, purification, and reflection. One can easily see in this lunar cycle the five steps for performing the conjuration of a spirit.

We have now covered everything that a competent Witch or Pagan should know and have in his or her repertoire in order to repurpose that expertise for conjuring spirits. Conjuration itself doesn't require any kind of massive expenditure, a collection of rare or obscure items, or learning methods and techniques that depart from the basic practices a Witch or Pagan might already possess. There are some new methods and techniques to learn, but these will fit seamlessly into practices that are already part of one's tradition and basic practice. While I have briefly described the nature of those basic practices and techniques in the preceding paragraphs, it would not hurt to succinctly state them here. There are eight basic elements that a Witch or Pagan should have as a foundational practice before considering adding the new techniques for summoning spirits. These eight elements are:

1. Consecrating sacred space, setting and empowering a magic circle

2. Adopting an open mind and cleansing it from cultural biases and prejudice

3. Practicing the methods and techniques of controlling consciousness as a periodic and regularly occurring discipline

4. Experiencing and even performing Godhead Assumption (drawing down the moon, horned god, or the sun)

5. Establishing a solid spiritual alignment with named and known deities

6. Regularly practicing divination techniques

7. Developing and practicing a spiritual and magical discipline, with daily, weekly, monthly, and seasonal workings and celebrations

8. Learning some astronomy and astrology—understanding the lunar and solar cycles

It is my belief that if the student has achieved some experience with these eight basic areas of spiritual and magical practice, he or she will be ready to learn the art of spirit conjuration. If by some chance the student is unknowing or weak in any of these eight areas, then he or she will know what to study and practice as a remedial exercise.

I must also assume that the student has additionally undergone some kind of initiation or self-dedication and has been practicing for a period of time. Mastery of these skills is not required, but understanding them and being competent in their practice is necessary. Just as it would be foolish to run away from home before becoming an adult legally and able to be self-sufficient, so it would also be foolish to embark on the study of spirit conjuration without a solid practical discipline and competent skillset.

Witchcraft and Ritual Magic: Nomenclature and Technique

Let your mind start a journey thru a strange new world.
Leave all thoughts of the world you knew before. Let your
soul take you where you long to be ... Close your eyes let your
spirit start to soar, and you'll live as you've never lived before.

ERICH FROMM

Now that we have repurposed spirit conjuration in Modern Witchcraft, our task is to modify these basic practices to easily and safely perform a spirit summoning. We will also discuss the important elements that extend the paradigm of Modern Witchcraft. By extending our paradigm, we are seeking to build a connection to the ancient craft of the Witch using modern magical techniques.

In this chapter we will discuss the nature of the spirit world, how it is organized and structured, and how the various spirits are arrayed within it. We will also discuss the basic magical symbols that are used as ritual patterns or structures to access that world. In order to enter the spirit world, we will modify the common Witches' magic circle so that it becomes a symbolic representation of the world of spirits itself. The definitions of invocation and evocation not only represent certain semantic differences, but they are distinctly different operations as well. It will be important for the practicing Witch to know when to use one instead of the other. We will also cover the basic meditation and trance techniques that will be used in the spirit summoning rite. Finally, we will discuss some of the more important facts associated with the godhead assumption since that is the core rite and discipline a conjuring Witch employs.

World of Spirit

The world of spirit is always present, surrounding us at all times and in all places. It coexists with the material world but most of the time human beings are hardly aware it exists. They might have a sensation, insight, premonition, or a vague sensory impression, but most of the time they are oblivious to it. A sensitive psychic may have the ability at various times to perceive this world and acquire impressions and even communications from it and its occupants, but never consistently. Only a trained practitioner can perceive this world whenever he or she desires. This is because the world of spirit can only be perceived through the "eye of spirit," as Ken Wilber has called it, a euphemism for specifically trained senses not based on either corporeal senses or mental constructs. The fact that the world of spirit and its various phenomena cannot be perceived with either one's physical senses or mental impressions makes it seem mostly isolated from human observation and even speculation.

Spirit phenomena are beyond the physical senses and even the artifices of mental cogitation. It occupies a distinct world wholly of consciousness, but it is beyond the mind and its various disciplines and structures. Human beings can only directly perceive this domain when they are in the higher states of consciousness, and then what they hear, see, feel, taste, and perceive is with an artifice that only vaguely resembles the aspects of the physical senses. This domain powerfully influences the human mind, however, as moments of profound realization, genius, insight, inspiration, visions, and déja vù would seem to demonstrate. We visit this world at times when we dream; artists, poets, musicians, and writers also appear to draw their inspirations from this world. We live intimately close to this world and it has a powerful influence over us, but we only seem to be aware of it during peak moments of inspiration or madness. Otherwise, we seem to live in a world that is empty of anything having to do with that quality of "otherness" that so characterizes the world and phenomenon of spirit as we toil in our mundane lives.

Human nature integrally consists of the triad of matter, mind, and spirit, and there is a physical world, mental world, and a spirit world. All these worlds are similar to each other, and also are actually one indivisible world. We human beings are the intersection of these worlds, so we quite naturally have the key to each. We can relate to the physical world through our mentally constructed sensorial perceptions; but it is a different matter to try to perceive spirit since it is above and beyond our normal mental processes. In order to perceive spirit, we must block or ignore our physical senses and remove from our minds the restrictions, biases, and expectations in order to see with the eye of spirit.

There are a number of methods and techniques to achieve the proper mind-state and self-induced trance is probably the easiest. Other methods include various techniques of ecstasy, such as drugs, alcohol, or extreme physical activity (dance, sex, etc.), or conversely, forms of sensory deprivation. Breath-control, intoning mantras, and other techniques generating a meditative state produce the proper mental foundation for establishing a trance state; this is the method we will be following in this work. Therefore, I can say without any hesitation that ecstasy is the key to the gateway of spirit whether achieved by deliberation or accident.

Another point I can state is that the spirit world is a model of our material and mentally conceived world. It occupies the same space as the material world, except that it is wholly within the collective conscious mind. It is highly mutable, changeable, and even protean. It takes our material perceptions and biases and uses them to produce a simulacrum of material space; but in truth, it is a place that is empty of physical space yet full of meaning and symbolism. The human mind can only speak of the spirit world using metaphors and analogies that are useful models but ultimately unreliable.

You should think of this world as similar to the world of your dreams. Sometimes your dreams seem to present the same material world you live in every day. Other times your dreams present a world that is startling different, even impossible and fantastic.

The spirit world is like an individual's dream world, except that it is a collective world determined by culture and heritage. When I say that spirits are symbolic beings that are both within your mind and outside of it simultaneously, I am referring to that ocean of the collective or shared consciousness of our culture and language within which we unwittingly reside. This is a very complex definition that ultimately fails to do the phenomena of spirits and the world they reside in much justice. Yet this will not stop us from gaining access to this world and engaging the beings that live within it.

We can gain a better understanding of how this world is structured by using the models fashioned ages ago before human history was ever recorded.[16] I am referring to the beliefs and practices of shamans around the world and throughout history, but these beliefs or their vestiges can be found in nearly every system of trance-based spiritual topology in existence, present or past.

---

16 This methodology has a name, and it is called *eschatology*, which is the study of the afterlife, the domain of the dead, and spirits in general. Christian theology added the concept of an ultimate end-time to this term that became its dominant meaning, although other polytheistic religions had an end-time as well.

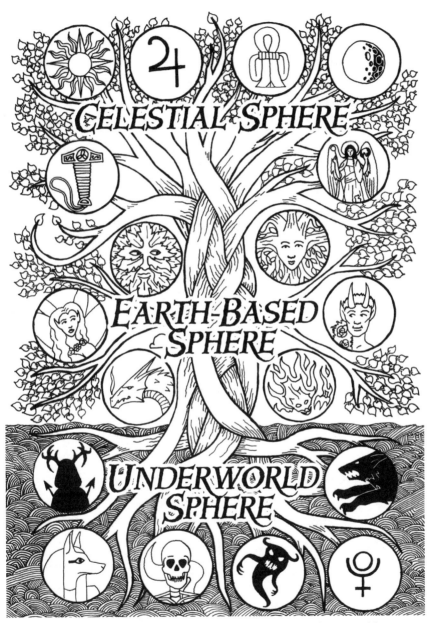

Figure 1: diagram of the three worlds and the linking bridge or world tree

Based on this library of symbols, the spirit world can accordingly be said to consist of three levels: the celestial heavens (sky and beyond), the local and greater geographic world (the earthly surface and all its features), and then the underworld (below the surface of the earth). While this is a simple and easily visualized structure, it is not the only one we can use. Often symbolic tables are used as a matrix to define the qualities and characteristics of spirits and beings to be found in the spirit world. These tables of correspondences could also be considered models for that world as well.

Various spirits, deities, demigods, ancestral ghosts, angels, demons, faeries, and earth-spirits as well as the symbolized and archetypal features of the sky (sun, moon, stars, clouds, storms, lightning, thunder), earth (trees, plains, rivers, lakes, seas, mountains, hills, valleys, deserts, forests, jungles, glaciers, etc.), and underworld (soil, roots, rocks, crystals, metals, caves, streams, ley-lines, tectonic faults, shallow and deep sea beds, volcanic intrusions, etc.) are collected into this world. In addition, we must include symbolic counterparts of all of the fauna, flora, and even mythic creatures, fantastic beings, and horrible monsters. It can be considered a very full and heavily occupied world, and we can see in these lists the effect it continues to have on the human imagination. However, it is a mystery as to whether the human imagination shaped this world or whether its elements and attributes shaped the way we perceive our mundane world. I would speculate that they have interacted within our minds Thus our mythic and imaginative stories and beliefs are the product of that interaction.

The three worlds are bridged by a great archetypal tree, mountain, rainbow, celestial roadway, ladder, or stairway. It unites the three worlds into a single world and allows passage between them. It also functions as a portal in this world to the spirit world. This bridge is also a symbolic metaphor for the spirit world as a whole. It also functions as the descriptive pathways or "ghost roads" that meander from our world into the varied and symbolic domain of spirits, caricatures (archetypal characters), and myths (stories). The gateway and bridge between worlds is a double portal, containing a doorway into that spirit world and a doorway that leads out of it and back into our world. Both doors are protected by a double-headed or multiple-faced guardian. Still, as a symbolic metaphor of the lintel threshold, gateway, bridge, or transformative passage, it is the focal point for self-induced trance which opens that world to the complete sensorial perception of the human traveler. It also contains the first spirit that Witches and Sorcerers must face, the Guardian of the Gateway. We will discuss this symbolic artifice, both the gateway and guardian, in greater detail when we describe the mechanism for performing the operation of summoning a spirit.

Since the spirit world doesn't have a physical basis in time and space as we would understand it, symbols and analogies are more important than anything else in that domain. That means that the symbolic identifiers associated with a spirit are very important to determine the identity, nature, and character of entities in that domain. Of course referring to a symbolic identifier is just a fancy way of saying that a spirit has to have a name. *An unnamed spirit is forever an unknown spirit*; so determining its name is critically important, for without a name, a spirit cannot be summoned.

Parts of the regimen of a conjuring Witch are the tools and mechanisms used to derive or determine the name of a spirit. Whenever a conjuring Witch encounters some spiritual being, she should ask it to identify itself. She can ask her familiar spirit godhead to retrieve the spirit's name, but she can also create a name and then adhere it to the entity. This is because it is in the nature of human beings to give everything a name, and this would also include spirits. We are the symbol makers since we use such constructs in our day-to-day use of language; it is a natural human proclivity. That attribute alone should give you an idea of the power that a single human being possesses who is fully and consciously immersed in the spirit world. Not only can we summon spirits and enter into the spirit world, we can also create spirits through the power of our imagination.

Names of deities, demigods, heroes, ancestors, and mythic creatures associated with one's spiritual and religious tradition are a part of the lore of a conjuring Witch. Additionally, there are the names from our cultural heritage that would include angels, demons, and the hosts of various occult spirits associated with the elements, planets, zodiac, the lunar and solar cycles, and of metaphysical models (like the Qabalah, or the World Tree, Magic Mountain, and so on). What doesn't typically have a name known to cultural heritage or traditions are local spirits of place and locality. As I have said, there are spirits everywhere and all around us. We live in a world filled with spirits, but most of them are local and associated with specific natural geographic features or flora, such as significant trees, hills, lakes, streams, rivers, ley-lines, etc.

All of these are features associated with a specific place residing both on the surface and under the earth. The actual physical features, what I call "topology," have a spiritual counterpart residing in the spirit world. They contain local deities and spirits associated with them, and it is the duty of the conjuring Witch to study and learn their names or attributes. A competent conjuring Witch studies her local setting and notes all of the unusual features of the land, and then visits and communes with them in order to learn about the local deities and spirits that reside within them. This is true whether you live in the city, the suburbs, or the country—each location has its own collective of deities and spirits to experience, learn, and to catalogue. (We will be discussing how to use trance walk and traveling in spirit vision into these domains later in this book, but first we need to focus on the mechanisms for conjuring spirits.)

A Witch who seeks to be a conjuring Witch must be the mistress of her locality, knowing, and being able to summon and engage spirits and deities associated with her home and its geographic place. In this manner she establishes her foundation and base. From there, she develops the confidence, mastery, and self-empowerment that allows her to take on the greater challenges that are to be found ever deeper in the spirit world. She starts out in the periphery in the spirit world counterpart of her home and progresses beyond the boundaries of her neighborhood and into the deeper and darker worlds of spirit. I would also recommend that the Witch discover and truly celebrate the spirits that reside in her home and are most intimately connected with her daily life. These spirits are as important now as they were in antiquity, known collectively as the Lares and Penates household deities.

How the conjuring Witch progresses in this knowledge is unique and different for each and every practitioner. It really depends on how they operate, whether cautious and steady or wild and risk taking. In the end, the distinction is not too important as long as the practitioner has obtained her familiar spirit or personal godhead. That relationship alone will be the guide and the guardian for this singular approach to summoning spirits and engaging with the spirit world.

There is an important thing to consider when discussing the nature and characteristics of spirits, and that is why they would want to allow themselves to be summoned and do the bidding of a human being. We already have some idea that the Witch is summoning the spirit for a specific purpose, but why would they bother to cooperate? Some spirits are emotionally cool, some warm, and others quite hot and volatile; some are readily helpful while others are hostile. Still, when called by a knowledgeable Witch they will appear. Why does this occur, and what are spirits getting out of the bargain of helping human beings?

If we consider that we are conscious beings functioning as a natural part of the spirit world and the material world then engaging with spirits is part of that natural process. Spirits gain a greater focus by being named and summoned and that helps them to evolve, which is just like people evolving when they gain knowledge through experience. Nothing stays the same and everything is dynamic. This means that the interaction between human beings and spirits is very important for their combined growth and benefit. So spirits, when properly summoned, will appear and interact with humans because it benefits them. They will help the Witch with her tasks who also benefits from contacting spirits and engaging with the spirit world—it really is a two-way street.

A spirit not only has a name but it also has a location or residence in the Spirit World; these combine to inform you about its nature. This is the first level for categorizing a spirit. Since there are three basic levels to the Spirit World there are three basic classes of spirits. These are celestial, earth-based, and underworld. Then there is a hierarchy of spirits from greatest to least. This hierarchy also follows the basic structure of three levels of the spirit world, although there are deities and demigods in all three interconnecting worlds. You might also notice that there are a number of spirits representing dead ancestors of some kind and they represent an important faction within the spirit world.

1. Major deities

2. Major demigods

3. Celestial intermediaries (all types)

4. Deities and spirits of celestial orbs (sun, moon, planets, zodiac, other stellar constellations)

5. Sky phenomena (deities and spirits personified as clouds, storms, wind, lightning and thunder, etc.)

6. Sky beings (winged creatures—lesser intermediaries)

7. Great ancestors, heroes, masters

8. Lesser earth deities and spirits (faery) of locality, also household deities and spirits

9. Underworld chthonic deities and spirits, lesser ancestors

10. Ghosts, mythic monsters, creatures of darkness

11. Infernal spirits and chthonic monsters (proto-earth formations)

A spirit's name is qualified by the class of spirits that it belongs to and its residence in the spirit world. This simple attribution begins the process of building up spirit name lists and qualities that become a complex interrelated set of tables—the *Liber Spirituum* or Book of Spirits. From the spirit's name additional information can be extracted, such as the meaning of the name (if any), the language that it is based on (if any), and the exact spelling in that language or a close phonetic equivalent. The name is used to craft a sigil or character glyph that represents the spirit's name through the artifice of a symbol.[17] The sigil is the important key or link used to access the spirit. Later on, the spirit can provide a more elaborate character or mark that uniquely represents it in a symbolic manner.

Other spirit attributes, such as the association or affinities with known qualities such as color, incense or perfume, gem stone, mineral, herb, etc., can be employed. There are also other affinities and associations such as the image or imago of the spirit (if it is known), its personality, character and style, likes and dislikes, its relationship to other spirits of the same class or to one that is superior and has rulership over it. There can be analogies to the four directions, elements, winds, seasons, the elementals, the seven planets, the twenty-eight mansions of the moon, the twelve signs of the zodiac, the thirty-six zodiacal decans, or the seventy-two zodiacal quinians. Spirit attributes, associations, or affinities can be determined by making an initial

---

17   The spirits of the seventy-two demons of the *Goetia*, the *Goetia-Theurgia*, and the *Ha-Shem Angels*, as found in the various grimoires and books of spirit magic, use what are known as "seals" to symbolize these classes of spirits. The seal would be used in place of a sigil, although a sigil would technically still work.

and preliminary contact with a spirit or through research and derivation from various published materials such as the old grimoires. As a conjuring Witch evolves and expands her practice, she can seek out source material about classes of spirits, hierarchies, and correspondences and other mythic lore from many sources depending on her interests and the guidance of her familiar spirit.

Over time, a conjuring Witch will possess all of the information necessary to summon and call a spirit into some semblance of manifestation. Imagine this catalog of information functioning like a person's little black book of potential hot dates. There would be a name, picture, cell phone number, street address, email address or Facebook profile, characteristics, clothing style, likes and dislikes, days and times available, and other important information, including even a diary of previous dates and what happened. The more information such a book contains, the more successful that a man or woman who possessed it might be in the dating scene. Not everyone would approach dating in this kind of organized manner, but those who did might keep themselves from making terrible mistakes or gaffes during a romantic date, particularly if they were dating more than one person. However, I would advise potential conjuring Witches to approach spirit summoning with that idealized degree of detail and discipline. This is because the results of such a working should be maximized to the highest level for the mutual benefit of both spirit and human being. When approaching the vast and convoluted world of spirit, why leave anything to chance?

Magical Symbols and Ritual Structures

This brings us to the topic of the power of symbols and how they impact consciousness to allow for the interaction between the body, mind, spirit, and the spirit world. These symbols have been incorporated into specific ritual structures so that they can be fully experienced on all levels of being. While there are some very complex elements and attributes of the spirit world associated with analogies and myths representing the various qualities and characters of spirits and their interactions, we will be focusing on the most basic and fundamental symbolic structures used to define their world and summon them. These structures are the circle, the square, the triangle, and the equal armed cross. These might seem almost too simple. Once you understand how important these simple geometric shapes are regarding the summoning of spirits then I think that everything will fall into place. These shapes, by the way, are also important for describing the domain of the spirit world.

When I use the words *symbol, device,* and *tool,* I am referring to something very specific in regards to magic and Witchcraft. A symbol is a sign; a device is where that symbol is drawn in the air with a wand or athamé; and a tool is an actual physical object, such as a pentacle necklace. A simple example is the pentagram: it is a symbol; and when it is drawn in the air with an athamé it is a device; and when inscribed on a round flat piece of metal, ceramic, or wood is a tool.

Another important symbol used in magic is the device of the Rose Ankh, which consists of the crux ansata or cross with a loop (signifying a pregnant cross or sandal strap) and a rose or spiral in its center. It is the feminine counterpart of the rose cross and is a symbol of eternal life resonating with the central rose of passion and love. While this formulation is used as a symbol of the Goddess and Her compassion and power of protection in some traditions of Witchcraft, it is also a magical device. In this way, it functions as the rose cross does in the Golden Dawn, being a symbol of the tradition, a magical tool, and a device used in a ritual such as the ritual of the Rose Cross. The Rose Ankh symbolizes the descent and incarnation of spirit into matter and the manifestation of spiritual grace and sacramental blessings. I have worked with this symbol quite extensively and have found it to be uniquely qualified to function as a religious symbol, magical tool and magical device drawn in the air.[18] It is an integral part of a summoning rite, as we shall see.

The symbolic quality of a circle is a world, because it represents the enclosed boundary for a separate place or a world within a world. When used in the Witches' magic circle, it becomes the boundary between the mundane and spirit worlds. Although the magic circle is warded or protected by the four watchtower dread lords and the principle deities, it can be expanded under certain conditions, bringing us to the next set of structures. Additionally, a magic circle can be set inside of an already existing magic circle, thereby producing a world within a world. This is also an important practical technique when a Witch needs to symbolically replicate the mechanism for generating the recursive quality of the spirit world within a complex magic circle structure. It assists the Witch to isolate and focus on a specific circular point within the magic circle.

While the traditional Witches' magic circle is aligned along the four cardinal directions where the watchtowers are placed, a more realistic structure would allow for more points of the compass than just four. As Modern Witchcraft is guided by an eightfold path (and there are eight seasonal celebrations), it would not be illogical or unwarranted to use eight compass directions instead of four. What I am proposing is a magic circle with four cardinal directions (north, east, south, and west) and also four in-between points that I call the angles (northwest, northeast, southeast, and southwest). We add the four angles to the four Watchtowers, producing a magic circle with eight nodes or points. In the center of the circle there are three additional points, which are also very important. The highest point in the center of the circle is called the zenith, the lowest the nadir, and the point between them is called the midpoint.

---

18   As far as I know, I am the only one who uses the Rose Ankh as a magical device in rituals. It is not something that was part of my Witchcraft tradition.

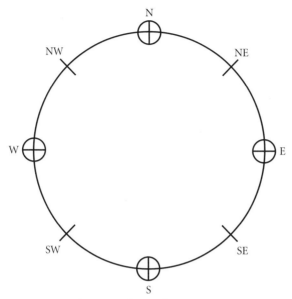

Figure 2: diagram of an eight-point magic circle

I have found that using eight points (with three points in the center) instead of four gives me a greater creative edge when designing ritual structures for elaborate and advanced ritual workings. There are other structures that can be incorporated into the formulation of a magic circle, such as the sixteen nautical wind directions. However, we can stick with using an eight-pointed circle with center points to perform spirit conjurations and gain entry into the spirit world.

The spiral is another important magical symbol, but I consider it to be an extension of the circle. A spiral has two basic qualities, direction and vector. Direction consists of either being deosil (clockwise) or widdershins (anti-clockwise). Vector is whether the spiral is moving to the center or to the periphery. Using these two dimensions, we can produce four distinct spirals, each having a separate meaning and function. Spirals are produced in ritual through waving a wand and drawing it in the air or by circumambulating the magic circle.

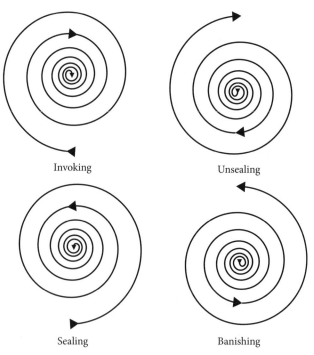

Figure 3: diagram of the four spirals

The basic spiral has a deosil direction and a vector of moving from the periphery (outside) to the center (inside). This spiral is called an invoking spiral because it draws energy into a focused center. An invoking spiral is used to focus the energy of a spirit or an energy field into a single point.

Conversely, a banishing spiral has a widdershins direction and a vector of moving from the center to the periphery. A banishing spiral releases energy built up into a point and sends it in all directions.

Less known are two other spirals used for specific kinds of ritual structures such as a vortex. We will be covering this ritual structure later, but we can at least say that a vortex cannot be banished, so it must be either sealed or unsealed. The last two spirals are for sealing and unsealing a vortex. The sealing spiral has a widdershins direction and a vector of moving from the outside to the inside, and the unsealing spiral has a deosil direction and a vector of moving from the inside to the outside.

However, when performed as a circumambulation in the magic circle, a sealing spiral produces an active energy structure called a vortex. This is the exact opposite of a cone of power, which is formed by a circumambulation of the magic using an invoking spiral. The sealing quality of the sealing spiral only functions as a seal when it is drawn over another device (previously drawn in the air) or a circle point such as an invoking pentagram or one of the watchtowers. This is also true regarding the other three spiral devices.

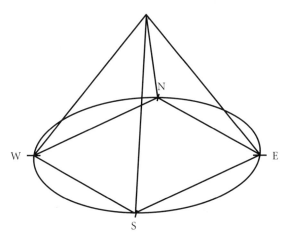

Figure 4: diagram of a circle squared & figure of the pyramid in the circle

The ritual structure of the square uses the pattern of the four points on the magical circle joined together with lateral lines of force to produce the primary symbolic artifice of masculine polarized power. Where the circle is archetypally feminine, the square is masculine. When used as a ritual pattern, the square is much more sharply defined and powerful than the cone of power, but it is seldom understood or used in most Wiccan ritual workings. When the square is erected within a consecrated magic circle, then it becomes the most elementary symbolic representation of the Great Rite—the joining of the archetypal feminine with the masculine. Squaring the circle automatically produces magical power, since it has a very paradoxical symbolic meaning, representing as it does an impossible problem in geometry.[19] This structure becomes even more interesting when it is brought into three dimensions using the zenith in the center of the circle as the point where a two-dimensional square becomes a three-dimensional pyramid. The prismatic ritual structure of the magic pyramid has as its base the square within the circle. So it draws from a powerful source of magical energy and pulls it into a singularity where the four corners merge at the zenith. When the four corners of a magic circle are defined with a specific element (or a combination of them by means of drawing an invoking pentagram) and these points are merged into union at the zenith of the circle, then the resultant prismatic energy field manifests as a glowing pyramid of varied lights. I have called this materialized ritual structure the Pyramid of Powers.

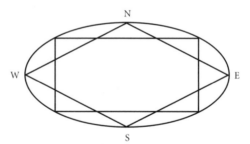

Figure 5: diagram of the octagon in a magic
circle & figure of two interlocking pyramids

---

19   Because of the transcendence of Pi, mathematicians have declared that exactly
     squaring the circle with a minimum of calculations is impossible, and so
     conversely is the act of circling a square. The square and the circle must have
     exactly the same volume. It is, therefore, a symbol of impossibility, which makes
     it the perfect representation of magical power.

Not everyone can conceptualize this energy structure; but it is tangible and produces an intensely stimulating force encapsulated by the magic circle. A sigil is then placed in the center of the circle that symbolizes the Witch's purpose and intent and the prismatic energy field is linked with it. All a Witch has to do at this stage is to put this force in motion (to exteriorize it). She focuses and draws on the power of the pyramid at the center of the circle, and then performs a circumambulation of the magic circle from the center spiraling widdershins out to the periphery of the circle. Once the spiral is complete then the energy field is released into the mundane world to do its work.[20]

The simplicity of this ritual pattern and its power and flexibility make it much more useful than the simple cone of power. It is for this reason that I prefer to use the pyramid instead of the cone. A more elaborate variation of this circle squared is where two squares are intertwined within a circle, thereby producing an octagon, or in three dimensions, two interlocking pyramids. You can see that there are endless possibilities with these various geometric energy structures, which I call prismatic energy fields.

As compelling as these ritual structures are for use in a conjuration, I won't be covering them in this work. While it is true that using such a ritual structure would aid in energizing and empowering a working, helping to make the spirit manifest in a more tangible manner, I feel that this topic is beyond the scope of what I would like to accomplish in this book. Even so, prismatic energy fields are not an essential element of summoning spirits since they are instead an essential part of the energy model of magic.

---

20 It helps for the Witch to pretend that there is a great deal of resistance encountered when pushing the power from the center of the circle to the outer periphery. The final steps of this outward spiral are expressed as an emphatic gesture, where the collective energy is projected from the circle out into the mundane world.

The energy model of magic proposes that there is an energy foundation to all things, and that this energy can be generated, targeted, and projected to cause objects, people, and events in the material world to be altered and influenced according to one's intention. Unlike the spirit model, this one assumes human beings have an innate power and capability far beyond what is considered normal and that this field of energy links everyone and everything together.

If this sounds a bit like "the Force" in *Star Wars*, it is not a coincidence. It is a typical borrowing of mystical precepts and a form of cultural appropriation that is found everywhere in modern cultures. While this model is very ancient and diverse (such as exemplified by the terms *mana* or *chi*), the methods used in Western magic are actually quite modern and recent.

If you want to know more about this other model of magic, you can examine one of my previously published works, such as *Mastering the Art of Ritual Magick.*

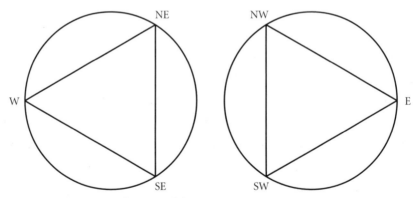

Figure 6: diagram of the Western and Eastern Gateway ritual patterns (left to right)

The symbolic structure of the triangle represents a doorway or gateway in the simplest geometric fashion. It is an enclosed plane figure with three straight lines and three angles. It also encapsulates the rule of three: *thesis, antithesis,* and *synthesis,* or using the symbols of myth: the *guide, guardian,* and the *ordeal.*[21] The triangle represents both the process of transformative change and the transition from one state to another or the passage between worlds. In order to open up the magic circle so its occupants might engage the other levels of the spirit world, the triangle is employed as a ritual pattern within the magic circle. The apex of the triangle always points to either the west or eastern Watchtowers, while the two legs of the triangle are set in the opposing angles. Thus the western gateway triangle points to the west, but its two legs would be fixed in the northeast and southeast angles. The eastern gateway triangle points to the east, but its two legs are fixed in the northwest and southwest angles. The gateway ritual pattern is set up *within* the magic circle, not on the outside as it is in ceremonial magic using what is called the triangle of evocation.

Once the gate is defined, the *passage* is made through the artifice of the pantomime of opening and passing through a curtained doorway. To close the passage, approach the gateway curtain that is already open and make the pantomime of closing it. There isn't a real curtain, of course, but the symbolic act of opening and closing an imaginary one defines the gateway structure as being either open or closed. Additionally, a western aligned gateway is the entrance to the spirit world, and an eastern gateway is the exit (coming forth into the light). We will be using the opening and closing of the western gateway for our work.

---

21 There are many other variations of the number three, and any of them can be used to qualify the mystic attributes of this number. A common ancient theme (Hindu) uses the concepts of creation, preservation and destruction, the three-fold Goddesses (like Hecate), or the Holy Trinity in Christianity.

Figure 7: diagram of the Rose Ankh

The Rose Ankh is a device that is drawn in the air like any cross device. However, the Rose Ankh device has a very special meaning and purpose for the conjuration of spirits, since it is a sign of protection (heart of the Goddess) and also it has the qualities of a magnetic energy that draws things to it. Because it symbolizes the incarnation of spirit into matter, it can also represent the drawing down of spirits into a focused point of manifestation. Therefore, it symbolizes the process of conjuring spirits. When set to multiple locations in a magic circle, like the four quarters, it will create a magnetic web that will attract and constrain spirits summoned by their name and sigil.

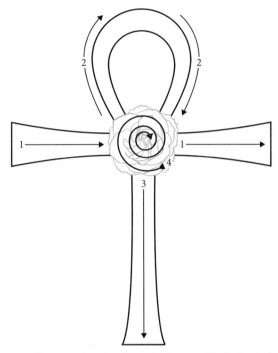

Figure 8: diagram showing how the Rose Ankh device is drawn

The Rose Ankh consists of two devices drawn in separate steps. The cross is drawn in the first three steps and then the spiral in its center is the fourth. The spiral represents the rose just as it does in the Rose Cross. The ankh is drawn with the hand or a wand (never an athamé) starting at the left arm of the cross, proceeding straight across to the right arm. Next is the loop, starting in the center point between the two arms and proceeding clockwise back to the center. The base is drawn starting at the center between the lateral two arms and proceeding down to the position at the foot of the cross. The spiral rose is drawn with an invoking spiral from just outside (bottom right) where the two arms connect proceeding to the very center of the cross, thus anchoring it.

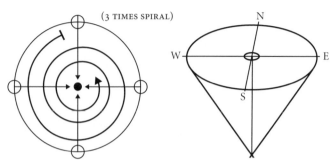

Figure 9: diagram of the Crossroads ritual pattern with vortex (left to right)

A crossroads ritual pattern is one of the more powerful symbolic ritual structures that a Witch can employ in a magic circle. There is a lot of folklore and mythic tales associated with the crossroads. It would seem to emulate not only a threshold crossing but also succinctly define the whole foundation of the spirit world. The crossroads represent a lintel or threshold passage and have many ancient antecedents, particularly in association with deities having chthonic or underworld qualities, such as Hermes, Hades, Persephone, and Hecate. It was believed (and still is in some cultures) that a crossroads denoted a transition point between the material and supernatural worlds. Even today, our language reflects this transitional nature whenever we say that someone (or something) is at a crossroads. A double crossroads occurs in many of the stories associated with the mythic "Hero's Journey" story, since there is an entrance portal as well as one to exit. One of the best sources for researching this theme can be found in Joseph Campbell's *The Hero with a Thousand Faces*.

Establishing a crossroads in a magic circle is easily accomplished and doesn't require travel to some remote location where two roads cross. Simply drawing the four Watchtowers together into a crossroads within a magic circle would dramatically change the whole quality of that ritual structure. All a Witch would have to do once a crossroads is established is put it in motion (to interiorize it). She would draw the four Watchtowers together using a sword and then perform a widdershins circumambulation from the outer periphery of the circle slowly spiraling into the center. This would draw all of the forces within the circle into the center and push it down into the nadir (the lowest point in the circle). The results produced from these ritual actions would produce a powerful vortex energy field that would contain everything established within it. I have compared it in the past to a "black hole," and from a purely magical perspective, it certainly acts like one. It also functions as a counterpart of the spirit world wholly encapsulated within the magic circle.

When the Rose Ankh is drawn to each of the four Watchtowers prior to drawing them together, the resultant energy field contributes a physical force that complements the symbolic quality of this ritual pattern. It creates a powerful magnetic container within which the operator may summon a spirit. I refer to this construct as the Rose Ankh vortex, and it is the heart of a summoning rite. As previously stated, a vortex cannot be banished; a sealing spiral is used instead.

As you have doubtlessly guessed, assembling these ritual structures together into a ritual working would give Witches and Pagans a powerful ritual structure for defining a double gateway and erecting a symbolic counterpart of the spirit world within the confines of the magic circle. When I have previously discussed the necessity of opening up a magic circle to engage with the whole of the spirit world, using these additional ritual structures is exactly what I had in mind. These ritual structures are simple, elegant, and quite succinct, and more importantly, they work exceptionally well. Let me quickly cover the sequence that these ritual patterns would be performed to prepare and set a magic circle for any kind of encounter or engagement with the spirit world and its denizens.

1. Make sacred space. Establish a magic circle with four Watchtowers erected and the tutelary Deities called. (This is the normal coven working environment. The practitioner could

also generate a cone of power or some other method of charging the circle like a pyramid.)

2. Set the four Watchtowers each with the Rose Ankh device and then draw the four Watchtowers together into the center of the circle. Charge it with a widdershins circuit of the circle—outside to the center and down to the nadir.

3. Establish a western triangular gateway and make a passage out of the protective environment of the consecrated circle and into the spirit world.

Performing these three steps is all a Witch needs to do to transform that basic protected and consecrated magic circle into a symbolic counterpart of the whole of the spirit world. A Witch manipulates the three central points in the center of the circle to determine what level of the spirit world she wishes to enter, but she should be able to access any part of it because everything within this world is interconnected. And to leave or depart the spirit world, she must seal the gateway and make the closing portal sign. At the end of this rite the Watchtowers would also be sealed, as once a vortex is erected in a magic circle it has a certain degree of permanence. (You don't use a banishing spiral to deactivate a vortex.) The normal circle closing rite that is typically used no longer functions as such, so another mechanism is used to end the working (sealing spirals).

We will of course go much deeper into the details of these ritual structures and even examine the outlines I will provide. These ritual structures are quite effective, but anyone who is seeking to use them should also learn to become competent at performing a godhead assumption, since that will be the only protection that a Witch might have once the other world is fully engaged.

Invocation and Evocation Defined

Now that we have described the domain of the spirit world and its occupants and revealed the ritual structures used to establish a symbolic counterpart of that world, we can further define what the words *invocation* and *evocation* functionally represent. We can show how they characterize two significantly different but not entirely opposing systems of conjuring magic.

I have already stated that invocation is to call from above and that evocation is to call from without or below. When we consider the three levels of the spirit world, we can broadly define an invocation as summoning a deity or a spirit that is located amongst the celestial hierarchy and an evocation as summoning forth an earth-based or underworld spirit. Additionally, we invoke our own special godhead that we assume and join to our being.

The difference between these two types of operations may appear to be subtle, but invocation does not require any kind of constraining, binding, and releasing. We don't, for instance, bind or constrain a deity since gaining the good will and favor of such a powerful being is our paramount purpose for summoning it. We also need to keep in mind that the actions of constraining, binding and releasing are not to be mistaken for any kind of aggressive hostility or coercion toward the target spirit. These three steps—constraining, binding, and releasing—represent the simple fact that the spirit must be formally summoned and brought to a specific focal point in order for it to manifest. The spirit is then fixed to a purposeful task (binding) and then released so that it might perform that task once the evocation rite is completed. This is why an invocation only requires three steps and an evocation requires five.

I listed the eleven different classes and levels of spirits in the World of Spirit section, and I can also further distinguish which of these classes generally are to be invoked from those that should be evoked. Deities and demigods are always invoked wherever they reside in the spirit world, the rest of the spirits follow this basic rule. The spirit classes from 1 through 5 are summoned by invocation, and the spirit classes from 8 through 11 are summoned by evocation.[22] For classes 6 (sky beings) and 7 (great ancestors), although they would likely be candidates for an invocation rite, they might require an evocation rite for summoning depending on their willingness to appear to the conjuring Witch. Spirits that are beneficent and good could be summoned using an invocation rite while spirits that are neutral, volatile, negative, or hostile would have to be summoned using an evocation.

When a conjuring Witch prepares for a spirit summoning, part of that preparation is to query and contact the spirit informally in order to determine its basic nature and attitude toward being summoned. Performing an informal summoning will also determine the mechanism for performing a formal conjuration. Through an initial contact, the Witch will know very quickly if the target spirit is going to require an evocation or invocation rite. Learning the nature of a spirit is part of the process of summoning it, and this alone is the best knowledge and information a Witch can discover about any spirit or class of spirits.

An invocation rite consists of three basic steps:

1. Preparation and consecration

2. Invocation

3. Communion

An evocation rite consists of the five basic steps previously listed:

1. Preparation and consecration

---

22   I would exclude household deities and spirits from this rule—they should be invoked but never evoked.

2. Invocation

3. Constraining

4. Binding

5. Releasing

We will discuss these two different ritual mechanisms in greater detail later in this book. We will also discuss how these ritual workings are to be employed within the fully established vortex counterpart of the spirit world, performed within the artifice of the magic circle, crossroads, and western gateway. All of these ritual steps and components are to be carefully assembled into a rite of invocation or evocation. The preparation for a summoning is probably the most important step. It always takes longer to carefully prepare for a summoning than it does to actually perform it.

All of these components that I have described above are a necessary part of the regimen of conjuring spirits; but the most important discipline that a Witch must develop is controlling consciousness. She must first produce the proper mental state so that the magic circle and all of the ritual patterns and energy structures become fully realized and accessible to her senses. This is accomplished through a light trance state. A deeper trance state is required for the godhead assumption that must accompany every entry into the spirit world and every conjuration. The Witch will vary the intensity of the trance state as she proceeds through the steps of the conjuration process, so developing a strict discipline of controlling consciousness is necessary for performing a formal summoning rite.

A trance state is built on the foundation of a solid meditation state; therefore the key to controlling consciousness is to build up a regular meditation practice. Trance is an easy state to reproduce and everyone experiences it to a lesser or greater degree every day. It is usually a nuisance to be overcome when it is important to be fully focused and aware, but in the case of long-distance driving it can be quite dangerous. However, for self-induced trance as it is used in conjuring, one must learn to make the trance state light or deep. This is not too difficult, but it does take some practice over time.

The regimen of controlling consciousness should have the basic form and incorporate the following elements in order for it not to be just a simple or shallow practice that the Witch performs prior to a working. What I am discussing here is the necessity of making this a regular, daily practice that becomes enforced and deepened over a period of time.

Basic Meditation Practice and Trance Techniques

A basic meditation practice consists of the following structured steps. These steps should be fully mastered and internalized so they become automatic.

1. **Posture**—If you are going to be sitting for a period of time without moving or fidgeting, you will need to adopt a sitting posture that is very comfortable. Some people can sit cross-legged for a long time comfortably while others need some kind of back support. However it is managed (e.g., using a meditation cushion or a chair) is not important—what is important is that such a sitting posture can be maintained from around ten minutes to a half an hour or more. The furniture needed for this meditation period should be an important part of the temple area.

2. **Breath-control**—There are a number of techniques used for controlling the breath and regulating it in some manner, such as the four-fold breath. However, these techniques are not as important as being able to completely focus your attention on the unrestricted breathing cycle. You should be able

to focus on your breathing to the exclusion of any thoughts, feelings, or other distractions.

3. **Mantra intoning**—This is where you take a word or just the simple "Aum" and begin by intoning it at a moderate volume and then allowing it to decrease until it is just a resonating humming. This is repeated over and over for a period of time.

4. **Concentration**—Learn to focus your mind on one thing and only one thing to the exclusion of everything else. This is a difficult task to master, but it only needs to be enforced for short periods of time. Try watching the second hand or the second display of a watch or use a timer and seek to exclude all other thoughts, impressions, or feelings. It is quite difficult, but you will note the duration of time that this operation was successful. If you can manage to do it for a couple of minutes, you are doing quite well. Later on, as this talent is developed, you can use it to meditate on a topic or word and passively observe anything the mind might reveal.

5. **Contemplation**—This can be approached in two different manners. In the Eastern traditions, one learns to empty the mind of everything, including all thoughts, impressions, and feelings. The other method is to focus on just a single concept or symbol while passively noting what transpires in exclusion to everything else. The easiest way to do this is to focus on your breathing without distractions while gently blocking all other thoughts or anything else that might cause an interruption. This can be done whether it is to focus on a single concept or symbol, or to fully empty the mind of all conscious thoughts. I recommend trying both types of contemplation.

6. **Mindfulness**—One of the most important elements of meditation is to learn the art of passive observation. If you are meditating and find yourself thinking about something else or even beginning to fantasize, just gently become aware of the lapse, break away, and then return to what you should be doing. Don't judge yourself or the quality of your meditation. Just accept everything as part of the natural process. This is a very important mental state to develop because it helps to establish a place of peace and detachment within you, and this is not only important for working magic but also learning to live with yourself and others.

These are the six elements you should use in developing your daily meditation session. Start out by assuming your comfortable posture then begin with your controlled or focused breathing for a time. Once you feel peaceful and at ease then try performing a mantra intonation for a period of time. After this is done, you can simply become very still and seek to completely empty your mind by only focusing on your natural breathing cycle. You should perform this meditation for fifteen minutes when starting. Once it becomes natural, you can extend it to thirty or forty-five minutes. You can either set an alarm to let you know that the time has elapsed or occasionally look at your watch when you feel you have met your meditation objective.

Another exercise you can perform is what I call the Body Scan.[23] This is done while lying completely down on the floor, couch, or bed, and assuming a restful breathing cycle. While focusing on that breathing cycle, you can begin to focus your attention on the toes of your left foot, feeling them without moving them. Then you can progress

---

23 This is a standard practice of the Mindfulness Stress Reduction methodology, and it works quite well.

up the body, from the toes of your left foot to the bottom of your foot including the ball, arch, heel, and ankle. You then progress up the foot, focusing on every part, to your knee, calf, and thigh. After that you start with the right foot, beginning at the toes and moving up to the thigh. Once both legs are fully scanned in this manner, you can proceed to the pelvis, hips, buttocks, lower to higher back, and then the torso, stomach, chest, heart, and then focus on the left arm, hand, and fingertips, the right arm, hand and fingertips, the neck, back of the head, and then your face, ending with the crown of your head. The idea is to slowly and methodically follow all of the points of the body from the feet to the crown, activating every part of your body. The challenge is to do this slowly and methodically without falling asleep or becoming distracted. You will find that keeping awake or undistracted while doing this is not easy to achieve, but the trick is to focus on your breathing while doing it. Performing the Body Scan produces a state that is both centered and grounded at the same time. I would introduce this exercise at the conclusion of any intensive meditation session or magical working to assist in the grounding process.

Once you have gained a certain amount of success at establishing and maintaining a meditation regimen, you can begin to practice trance induction. It is important and also simpler to acquire a trance state while having already established a good meditation state as the foundation. So, you can and should practice trance induction once your mind is in the peaceful and detached mental state produced by meditation. Trance is simple to adopt because it can be done by focusing the eyes on a specific object or point and maintaining that focus by staring at the object with a minimum of mental or physical distractions. This means gently suppressing the physical need to blink the eyes too often and looking without trying to interpret what you are seeing. Using this simple technique will enable you to adopt a trance state. Once you have entered that state, you can close your eyes and focus inwardly or continue to stare. There is a point where staring won't make the trance any deeper, so it becomes important to close the eyes and internalize this process. The key is to allow the trance state to develop itself while seeking to gently block any interfering or distracting thoughts or sensations.

Focusing the eyes on an object without trying to interpret what you are seeing is the key to acquiring a trance state. Once the trance state is acquired then you can close your eyes and focus inwardly. It is at this point where the trance state can be deepened or kept relatively shallow. If, for instance, you close your eyes only briefly and then open them, you will still feel the effects of the trance state, but it won't be as deep. You can also focus your eyes on a picture or poster that has certain psychedelic qualities in order to deepen the trance state. This picture or image is called a yantra in Hindu meditation practices. Another technique is to focus on the image reflected in a mirror, looking deep into the reflected image of your eyes looking back at you. One thing that can be done when using a mirror is look at your reflection and attempt to see the god/dess within, which would be an excellent precursor to godhead assumption.

As you work and experiment with trance states, always keep in mind that you are in complete control. You are deliberately inducing the trance state and therefore you can come out of it whenever you wish. Since no one is hypnotizing you, no one is placing their will over your own. You control this process from beginning to end, so you don't need to fear about going into a trance state and not being able to return from it. Trance states are a normal part of the cycle of consciousness and unconsciousness, just like sleeping and dreaming. However, sometimes it is prudent to use a timer with an alarm that will help you to surface after a period of trance. I would recommend using this kind of device for both meditation sessions of a fixed duration and also trance work when you are beginning to practice these techniques. After a while, these practices will become as natural to you as everything else in your daily life.

You should regularly practice these techniques and establish a powerful internalized mechanism that allows you to assume a meditation state or a trance state quickly and easily. Mastering this art of controlling consciousness will help you to perform more complex workings, such as fully realizing such transformative actions as entering into the spirit world. It can also help you to assume a specific deity or perceive the actual manifestation of the energies generated in the magic circle, revealing the hidden world of magical lines of force, deities, and spirits.

Godhead Assumption and the Votive Cult of the Personal Deity

The keystone to the whole overall process of conjuring spirits is the assumed deity that acts as the Witch's familiar. While meditation and trance assist the Witch in establishing the proper mind state for performing and realizing the operations of spirit conjuring, it is the assumption of godhead that truly crowns this process as one that is divinely guarded, guided, and blessed. Each spirit conjuring operation is represented by a full sensory immersion into the spirit world, and such a venture cannot be successfully achieved unless it is sanctioned by one's personal aspect of deity. This may sound like an unusual proposition, to have and work with a personal aspect of one's deity, but it is an integral part of building a personal connection with an external and publically known god or goddess.

Therefore, part of the discipline of conjuring spirits is to also perform the assumption of godhead rite and to establish a personal cult of that deity. Like meditation and trance, this rite is performed on a regular basis even when no magical operation is planned. The Witch should perform this rite during the monthly cycle of the moon, making it part of a weekly discipline. When first engaging with this aspect of deity, it is important that the Witch perform this operation often, perhaps starting with a daily practice until it becomes an automatic process.

In addition, the Witch should also perform the other elements of spiritual alignment on a regular basis along with godhead assumption. She does this so that she becomes very deeply connected with this personalized godhead until it is as much a part of her as any other internalized characteristic. It is important for the Witch to choose a god or goddess to whom she feels the greatest affinity and then she should build up a body of lore consisting of devotions, poetic hymns, invocations, periodic offerings, and also a regular form of sacramental communion. She builds up a rigorous and detailed liturgy to this personalized deity so that it becomes the primary focus of her spiritual and magical work. The focus of this activity is built up into a living shrine where all of the regalia, offerings, and symbolic vestments of this deity are placed, including a statue or idol that depicts it in an idealized form. Worshipping this personalized deity could be considered a narcissistic preoccupation, representing a regressive over glorification of the self, but it actually causes the self to be transcended as long as this self-worship is focused strictly on the deity and not on one's outward identity.

What we are talking about here is not the god or goddess X of a certain cultural pantheon, but it is the necessary starting point for such a development. After a short period of time, this known deity of a specific cultural lineage becomes the personalized godhead and the divine extension of the self, representing the highest aspect of that self as the god/dess within. As I have already stated, each and every one of us has within us a facet of the deity that is also one and the same with the unified source of all deities—the one absolute spiritual source. It is through this divinity that lives within us that we are able to sense, experience, and understand both the domain of Deities and spirits. The more activated and aware that we become of our own internal divinity, the more our conscious awareness is expanded and the more spiritually evolved we become.

So, working magic through the guise of a godhead assumption causes incremental but powerful changes to occur within the mind and soul of the Witch. She cannot help but be potently influenced by this godhead assumption and thereby ultimately ascending to the level of being fully aware and awake within the consciousness of her personal deity. While Modern Witchcraft may count and credit only one to three traditional rites of initiation, performing this kind of magic would produce a state of constant and continuous growth, representing a continual state of initiation. Each conjuration would be a transformative ordeal that would challenge and empower the Witch, and the successful outcome would expand her awareness and deepen her internal knowledge and insight. To conjure spirits and traffic with the Spirit World causes the Witch to become empowered, spiritually awakened and wise in the way of the mysteries of life and death. It would also awaken the inner godhead that would make her realize her own divinity within her mortal existence.

This process of ascension is not an egotistical expansion of the petty self. To be truly aware equally of the nature of the divine within the material and spiritual worlds as well as within oneself is also to be humbled by something that is vastly beyond any individual. If godhead assumption causes the Witch to become egotistical then what is occurring is not progressive nor transformative; it is instead regressive and a sign of mental instability. This is because the wisdom of true spiritual knowledge based on experience reveals the fact that individual humans are only a facet of the whole; the godhead living within them also lives within all animate and inanimate things. We are therefore all connected together with all of the other living beings, but no one part or individual is greater than any other. This fact is very humbling and grounding indeed. Thus, a true realization of the inner deity will not amplify one's sense of worth or status (which is the petty ego), but instead causes one to feel humility, knowing how everything is connected to the whole and is therefore, equal.

While it is true that we are exalted by the revelation of our inner deity, we are also humbled by the vastness of the totality of that divine being acting as the unified source of everything and everyone. That divine union, the totality of all being, is accurately symbolized by a circle whose center is everywhere and whose circumference is nowhere. The realization of deity is a paradox, and it represents the greatest mystery that anyone can encounter. It is also something that is central to the continual practice of spirit conjuration. A Witch who has mastered the conjuring of spirits has also plumbed the mysteries of spirit and deity itself; such an achievement is profoundly significant.

Engaging with spirits and deities has a transcendental effect on the conjuring Witch, even though her real intention is to purposefully summon spirits and freely enter into the spirit world. However, the personal godhead cult of the conjuring Witch is the most important part of learning to master this discipline, so we will be focusing on it in much greater detail in the next chapter.

How-To Guide for Practical Conjuration

We have covered the basic components of what is required to actually perform the art of summoning spirits; although this chapter and the preceding one have built on what is generally known already about practicing Witchcraft as a system of magic. All of these topics have been covered briefly, and now we need to focus on the specific tools and mechanisms that are used to summon spirits and engage with their world. I will discuss these topics in greater depth and give some basic outlines so that you will be able to write and assemble your own rituals and practices. This will allow you to fully immerse yourself into the spirit world and to call, summon, and communicate with spirits and deities. You will be able to do all of this because you will be completely protected, guided, and assisted at all times by your higher-self godhead as familiar spirit.

Mastering the godhead assumption rite is the preeminent task for the would-be conjuring Witch. We will cover the structure of this rite and we will also discuss all of the preparations needed so that you will fully realize your own personal deity. We will also cover all of the tasks and the discipline needed to establish a credible and continuous presence of this deity that will be tangible and accessible. Maintaining a spiritual alignment is one of the most important responsibilities that a conjuring Witch can take upon herself. I will give you everything that you will need to fully realize your personal godhead.

However, aside from mastering the rite of godhead assumption, you will also have to learn to see, hear, and feel the subtle and vague impressions of the Spirit World and understand clearly what is being communicated to you. You can employ divination tools to help you acquire this knowledge, but you also need to learn to fine-tune your senses to really understand what is communicated directly to you by spirits as well as how to communicate back to them. You should over time be able to hold a conversation with a spirit as you would a physical person, even though such communications will be in your mind.

Learning to build a magical link to the target spirit is another important technique that will be covered, since without the name and sigil or character you will not be able to fully summon and manifest a spirit. There are some simple tricks and techniques for producing a sigil based on the spirit's name and we will cover these techniques in detail.

Once all of these techniques are developed, you will need to know how to build up and prepare for either an invocation or an evocation. As I have said, the preparation work is the most important part of performing a summoning. We will go through every step and task required to build the proper foundation for summoning spirits.

Additionally, I will go over the three or five basic steps for an invocation or an evocation and give detailed instructions, including some ritual outlines and examples so you will be able to produce your own rituals. It is at this point where all of the components previously discussed and examined are assembled together to produce a complete system that will successfully result in a full spiritual manifestation. It is my hope that when you finally perform this rite for yourself that you will have developed your spiritual senses to a point where you will be able to both see and hear the spirit that you summoned. Otherwise you will have to perform divination in order to communicate.

Finally, we will examine (in the appendix) the top twelve grimoires which are now in various printed editions. These published works are available to examine and study. You can also appropriate any sigils, seals, spirit lists and descriptions, or anything else that strikes your fancy. Because this is an optional overview, you can find it in the appendix at the back of the book. Since you will already have a complete system for invoking or evoking spirits, you can treat the grimoires as optional lore that might be useful or adaptable for your magical regimen. We will cover the history, availability, and the lore found within each grimoire that might be most useful to you. Of course these opinions will be my own and they will be subject to your review and examination, if you choose to do so.

That is my plan for the rest of this book now that the basics have been briefly covered. I would like to invite you to move forward with me and learn about the details you will need to know to be a fully empowered and practicing conjuring Witch.

Building the Tools of the Modern Conjuring Witch: Part One

The expectations of life depends on diligence; the mechanic
that would perfect his work must first sharpen his tools.

CONFUCIUS

In order to make the transition from a modern traditional Witch to a full-fledged conjuring Witch, you will need to make some basic tools and add these to your repertoire for practicing Witchcraft based magic. As I have said previously, you don't need to go out and purchase a lot of expensive equipment or books in order to begin building up this extension to what you already have been practicing. None of this is either new or a radical departure from what would be customary for you, and in fact it is all quite practical. As they say, the devil is in the details, and we will now begin to review the major areas of this topic in greater detail. I will explain to you how to build some rites and practices that are not to be found in the typical Book of Shadows.

This chapter will cover the first two of the four basic objectives, and all of these tasks are related because they represent what must be done to prepare for any invocation or evocation. The first time that you go through this process there will be a lot of work and time required so that you can become competent at performing these preparatory tasks. In fact, I would say that until you are competent at these tasks you should not attempt to summon any spirits. The first two of these four objectives, which are covered in minute detail here, are:

Godhead Assumption—We will cover all of the steps necessary for you to determine your own inner godhead, and how you should assemble a ritual so you can fully assume that godhead into your own being. Included with this section are all of the ancillary rites and practices that will help you to establish and maintain the presence of that personal deity in all of your magical and liturgical workings, particularly in that special place where your godhead shrine is erected.

Controlling Consciousness—After having briefly gone over the techniques of meditation and trance, we will discuss how to apply these techniques so that you can begin to sense the spirit world under certain and controlled situations. I will discuss how you can learn to see, hear, and feel the nearly invisible spirit world and its occupants, spirits, and deities. I will also demonstrate how you can use dice to get answers when your senses fail to give you an adequate sense of the spirit or to communicate with it.

The first two objectives represent the backbone of any kind of conjuration working, which is to assume one's personal godhead and to keep that mind-state active as the magical working is performed. Controlling consciousness is also a key skill that has to be developed until it is an automatic process that one can assume and project at will. In fact, mastering these two processes is fundamental to any kind of magical working. They also go hand in hand, because without the ability to assume an effective trance-state one would not be able to properly perform a godhead assumption or to hear, see, and sense things in the spirit world. Both of these abilities are essential to function as a conjuring Witch, which is why they should be carefully and methodically studied and practiced.

Let us now begin to reveal all of the tasks that you will need to perform in order to become properly prepared to conjure spirits.

Godhead Assumption

We have briefly covered this topic in the previous chapters of this book, but now we are going to discuss all of the details that you will need to know to perform this rite and maintain the presence of this personalized deity within your home and throughout all of your magical work. This is unlike anything that you have been challenged to perform previously within your basic tradition, since it is the deliberate appropriation of Witchcraft liturgy used for personal and magical gain.[24]

This may sound like something that is technically forbidden in what might be construed as the classical or traditional version of Modern Witchcraft, and indeed it certainly bends the rules.

Typically, the assumption of godhead, referred to as the Drawing Down rite, is used by the High Priestess, High Priest, or some qualified surrogate to facilitate the mystery of the immanent presence of the deity for the benefit of the coven or grove. It is not supposed to be performed to empower or exalt the person who is responsible for this sacramental occurrence.

---

24 Of course, when we look at the Drawing Down rite that Gardner handed to his followers, we will see that it is in fact a derivation of the Golden Dawn godhead assumption rite. I suspect that Gardner purloined that rite, as he did numerous rituals, and repurposed it for his Witchcraft cult.

When I have talked to people about this use of the godhead assumption rite as performed by the individual for the exclusive benefit of that individual, some of my Witch friends have balked at this repurposing. Some have said that it should be the exclusive property of the elders of a group, clan, or tradition. I don't agree with this sentiment because engaging with the presence of the deity is something that all Witches and Pagans should experience for themselves and even by themselves. When we consider that each and every one of us has within a deity that is seamlessly connected to the Source, which is also known as the One, then activating that aspect in ourselves couldn't possibly be something unwarranted or unsanctioned.

Additionally, I have shown that the Witches' familiar of antiquity is similar to what today we would call our higher self or inner deity. That alone should dispel any protestations from traditional Witches that somehow performing the godhead assumption is a bad thing. I will assume that my readers desire to master the art of spirit conjuration, and this is the technique that I am proposing so that it will be accomplished safely and effectively. If you want to develop this skill then you will have to break the supposed rules that some have written to keep for themselves what should be a sacred obligation for all.

Before we cover the ritual of godhead assumption we should discuss some other important items that will determine the formulation and ultimate character that this rite will have once it is fully developed. Namely, if you seek to perform a godhead assumption then there is the formality of determining and selecting a deity you can assume. I can't, of course, tell you what deity to focus on, but I can at least help you make that determination if you are at a loss as to what deity to choose. The question can be put very simply, as it is in the Afro-Caribbean traditions, "What is the god of your head?" How do you determine the nature of the god within you? Who is that deity residing in the core of your being, waiting to be discovered? If you have no idea at all, then some divination would be helpful. Often simply asking the question and then meditating on it can begin to reveal the answer to this mystery. However, the divination that you should use to plumb this mystery should be much more detailed and extensive than simply throwing some dice. You will need to use tarot cards, rune stones, or some other more complex divination system. This is not an issue that can be resolved with the simple throw of the dice nor is it one that should be taken lightly. This task might even take some time to resolve, particularly if you have little or no information about the deity residing within.

In most cases, a Witch or Pagan has a certain affinity for some specific deity or cultural pantheon. It may even be that more than one deity attracts you, but through research and careful self-analysis a single deity can be selected to fit the Witch's character and personality. This fit between types, comparing the mythic character of the deity and your own personality, can be a matter of choosing a godhead like yourself or one who is the opposite. The chosen deity could even be the opposite gender (as it is with me), and in that case the Witch would approach her God as a mortal lover. The most important tool is the imagination, and the Witch should spend time not only collecting all of the known characteristics, likes, dislikes, and all the mythological stories where this deity is famously depicted, but she should contrast that information with the elements and life-story of herself. We are talking about creating a personalized version of the deity, and it becomes personalized when these two categories are merged—the mythic god and the Witch's persona.

Another important element that must be added to this contrast between personalized deity and human devotee is love. This sentiment might start with an affinity; but it needs to become a powerful attraction and an even stronger identification. It is a critical part of this working that what you have researched and assembled together about your chosen deity represents an entity that you love and can easily give all of the focus, all of your devotions, and all of your service to it. The very image that you have derived of this deity should be one that is attractive and even glamorous. This is because love is the binding cord that will draw and fuse this image of the godhead into your being, causing both to become one and the same over time. To facilitate this process of union, you will function as both the chief celebrant, priest or priestess, and even the congregation for the edification and worship of this deity. It must therefore be a private affair and one that you perform alone without any help or interfering distraction.

You will have to determine a focus for this devotion and worship, and that will be in the form of a painting, poster or better yet, a statue of some sort. It could also be something abstract, but a human likeness does make it easier to form a direct relationship with the image or idol of your elected deity. While it could be considered appropriate to consecrate this image, quite simply by using it over time you will make it into a fully empowered icon, for that is what it is.

Once you have acquired an image, you will need to select a proper place where it will preside. That place is the beginning of your shrine. You can also collect and use other items to embellish this shrine to make it beautiful and appealing. However, you will need devotional candles, incense holders, flower vases, and other implements to make offerings such as small plates and a cup. You can erect a table to hold these items or you can use a suitably sized wall niche, although a small table is more practical. The color of the cloth covering the table and other decorations should all be identifiable as being the colors, designs, and symbolic representations that you have researched and uncovered about that deity. Once this shrine has been assembled, you will need to serve this shrine on a periodic and continuing basis. You will focus all of your meditation and trance sessions and the various required liturgical operations on that shrine. You can even just sit before the shrine and let yourself feel love, adoration, and submission to this deity.

To build up a proper alignment to this deity you need to perform a series of liturgical rites on a regular and periodic basis. We should now discuss these operations in detail so that you will know what you are expected to do. All of these exercises are to be performed before you finally get to the point of performing the godhead assumption and communion rituals. The other operations are a necessary foundation to those final and crowning rites. Of course, once you graduate to the point of performing the godhead assumption for the first time, it will have to become something that you do regularly and often, perhaps once a week for a month or more. It needs to become an automatic process so that merely performing the basic gestures of this rite will produce the desired assumption.

Rituals of Alignment

1. **Devotions and Offerings:** You should give offerings of flowers, incense, and special food and drink to the deity on a regular schedule. Your research will give you an idea of what kinds of incense, flowers, beverage, and food to offer. Prior to giving new offerings, you should properly discard the old ones, giving them to the earth. You should find a spot outdoors where you can place these discarded offerings and where the elements and creatures of the earth can consume what is left. You should never partake of any of these offerings—they belong to the deity. Starting out, I would give offerings to the deity at least every three days. When you make these offerings, you can also light the candles for the shrine for the period of time representing your devotion. (One hour should be plenty of time.) Additionally, you can also burn incense every day or even more than once a day.

2. **Invocations and Summoning the Deity:** Once or twice a week you should sit or kneel before your shrine, make offerings, and then either recite or read out loud poetic hymns, paeans, and other types of devotional writings. I would recommend that you wear something over your head as a sign of piety (prayer shawl or hood), and that your clothes are newly laundered and that you have recently bathed and anointed yourself with perfumed oils. You should also recite or read invocations to the godhead, calling and exhorting that blessed entity to descend upon its image and appear before you in all its glory. This should be followed with a period of silent meditation and an adoration of the deity's image. As you get closer to the time where you will be performing the godhead assumption, this practice can be performed more frequently.

3. **Sacrificial Offerings:** All of the items and implements including the offerings themselves are gifts given to your personal deity representing your devotion and willingness to sacrifice resources and time in its honor. However, you can also consider giving occasional costly gifts (jewelry) and other cultic items (musical instruments, drums, bells, masks, vestments, weapons, etc.) to the deity. These should be given during a special offering presentation where you can offer them as a sign of your true devotion. The regular offerings are expected since they feed and empower the presence of the deity, but special offerings are to be considered very blessed gifts. This is particularly true if they represent some kind of redirection of resources that is not part of your usual outlay. These instances are where you are sacrificing something from your livelihood in order to give to the deity. A sacrificial gift can also be where you give up some habit, like smoking cigarettes, and then save that money to purchase a suitable gift for the deity.

4. **Regular and Periodic Service:** All of the services that you perform to keep the shrine clean, orderly, stocked with incense and supplies, and also the cyclic tasks of devotions and offerings represent a specific service to the deity. That service will certainly have an important value, since the more dedicated and constant you are, the greater the ultimate presence of the deity will manifest.

5. **Meditation and Trance Sessions Focused on the Shrine:** Once you have a shrine fully developed and you are performing periodic tasks to maintain it, you can also perform your daily meditations and trance practice sessions fully engaged and focused on the shrine. It is very appropriate to practice your trance sessions focusing on the image of the deity, and inwardly calling and summoning him or her.

6. **Lunar Cycle Represents the Liturgical Calendar:** During this period of building up the presence of the deity, you should coordinate your activities with the waxing and waning of the moon. Special devotions should be performed for the four points of the lunar cycle—new, first quarter, full, and the last quarter. The lunar cycle will be very important when you graduate to the point where you are performing invocations and evocations.

7. **Spiritual Service to the Community:** In some manner, however significant or humble, you should perform some kind of volunteer service to the community at large. It can be to your Pagan/Witchcraft community or even better, to your local community. When you are about to perform this volunteer service, you should announce it during one of your devotional offerings so that the deity will know that you are doing this service in his/her name. You shouldn't tell anyone why you are

doing this service, since it is to be an offering of devotion to the deity. By doing this, you will be bringing the private devotion that you are giving to this godhead into the larger world.

Once all of these actions listed have been incorporated into your spiritual and liturgical practices, then you can consider scheduling and planning for your first godhead assumption. We will now proceed to discuss this ritual in greater detail. The godhead assumption rite that I will be presenting here also includes a communion rite as well. This is where food and drink (or nearly anything) are blessed by the deity and then shared with yourself. Later on, you can use the power of making sacraments to bless and empower magical tools as well as sacramental offerings that can be used to sacralize one's working space similar to the Catholic use of the benediction rite.

A simple measure that you can use to determine if you are ready to undergo the godhead assumption rite is that when you perform your devotions and meditations before your shrine you can feel the presence of the deity residing there. When you recite invocations and call to the deity to appear you will begin to sense a numinous presence and perhaps will even hear a voice talking to you or at the very least making some kind of effort to communicate to you. You will also start having unusual dreams, paranormal sensations at odd times, premonitions, and a continuous awareness of the presence of the deity even when you are away from home. If you don't yet hear any voice speaking words inside your head, you can use your dice to receive answers to simple yes or no questions. Low numbers can equal negative answers and higher numbers are positive. Simple yes or no questions can help you develop the communication link between you and your personalized deity if there is no actual internal contact.

You will use the selected hymns, poems, and the invocations that you have researched and developed to build up the godhead assumption, since these texts have already been used to worship and make manifest the presence of the deity. Since you have been coordinating your devotions and offerings with the lunar cycle, you will schedule your first godhead assumption to occur just before the Moon becomes full.

It should be a day completely reserved for this work and nothing else. You will also need to schedule it at a time where there won't be any distractions or other people around who might interfere with what is being done. The entire day from when you wake up until when you retire to the temple should be dedicated to this work. If possible, plan for the actual working to be late enough at night where the neighborhood around you will be mostly asleep.

Plan the day of the working to be filled with performing devotions and offerings, since you will want the presence of the deity to achieve its highest manifested expression when you perform the assumption rite. Eat sparingly and lightly, and keep yourself actively engaged with your devotions, even while performing very mundane work such as bathing, making food, etc. Everything you are doing is exclusively for the deity. Prior to performing the assumption rite, you should spend a period of time in deep meditation, and from there into an even deeper trance state. Once this long meditation and trance session are completed, you can consecrate a magic circle and begin to perform this rite. Here is the outline of this ritual, giving you a clear idea of its contents and structure. This outline should be developed until it is complete, and then where permitted, memorized.

Rite of Godhead Assumption

This is the basic outline for the rite of godhead assumption. It starts out as an elaborate focused rite but over time and repetitive practice it can become internalized and then performed automatically and internally whenever required. The celebrant is the one who is performing this rite.

Preliminary Meditation

The celebrant meditates and begins to internally summon the personalized deity, called the godform. Feelings of devotion, worship, and love are projected into its image residing in the shrine.

Centering the Self

Celebrant stands in the center of the magic circle with arms down at the sides and performs a centering exercise—imagining seeing a bluish energy focused and moving up the special body points from foot, knee, groin, breast to crown in an ascending projection.

While this is done, the breath is drawn up into the body, held, and then exhaled gently through pursed lips while the celebrant holds her arms above her head, allowing the fingers of her hands to shake and vibrate.

Primary Invocation

Celebrant intones the primary invocation that consists of words establishing the image or imago of the deity, describing in great detail its appearance and characteristics. This can be memorized or read, but eventually it should become automatic.

As this is done, the celebrant should actually sense the godhead entity materializing before her. In addition, she positions her arms to form right angles, with the elbows against the sides of her body, and the arms straight out with the palms of the hands facing up.

This is the symbolic receiving pose, which indicates that the celebrant is ready to receive the spirit of the godhead.

Second Centering

Celebrant performs the centering exercise again, except this time the direction of the energy flow is descending, from the crown, breast, groin, knees, down to the feet.

This action draws the imago of the deity that was generated by the invocation down into the self.

Mantle of Glory

Celebrant draws an equal arm cross on her torso, aligning the power points visualized there so that a cross of blue light is formed upon her body at four points—head, groin, right shoulder, left shoulder.

At this point the imago that was drawn down is now powerfully linked and bound to the body of the celebrant.

Secondary Invocation

Celebrant begins to summon the deity into manifestation within herself. This is done by the following symbolic actions.

The celebrant intones a second invocation or summoning. Unlike the first invocation, this one summons, begs, entreats, and implores the deity to descend into the celebrant's body.

A triangle is drawn upon the body using the points of the left, right breast of the torso and the groin as representing a triangle.

A triangle is used because it establishes a gateway (with the heart as its center) where the deity will enter into the body of the celebrant, passing through from its celestial domains into her heart and soul.

Projection of Deified Self

Celebrant performs the centering exercise for a third and final time, and like the first time, the direction of the energy flow is from the feet to the head and beyond, done with a flourishing of the hands and ascending projection.

During this action, the celebrant internally summons the deity, repeating its name over and over as this exercise is done with deliberate slowness and with the greatest intensity so that it reaches a climax at the end, where its potency is felt throughout one's being.

With the arms fully raised and the eyes to the heavens, the celebrant wills herself to be the godhead, internally repeating the mantra—"I am so-and-so, the deity X" in such a manner that it becomes momentarily fully realized.

COMMUNION WITH THE DIVINITY

At this point the godform is fully assumed by the celebrant, and she may exult in the feelings of personal empowerment, alignment, and spiritual ascendency. She may sit down to momentarily stabilize this moment in her mind (especially if this is the first time) or she may perform various tasks in the guise of the deity. This would include consecrating food and drink, which she blesses with her hands and lightly blows her breath upon them.

FINAL GESTURE

After the godform has been assumed and fully experienced, it is important to meditate upon the imago of that deity and send feelings of thanksgiving and a loving farewell. As a token of respect and devotion, some kind of offering should always be left behind for the deity, perhaps even placed on the shrine.

Most of this rite consists of ritual actions and there is only a small amount of dialogue that needs to be written to complete it. Of course the most important part of this rite are the two sets of invocations and these will have to be researched and written up before it can be used. I would recommend that the invocations should be short and succinct so that they can be easily memorized.

Once this ritual has been fully developed, practiced, and used a number of times, it can then be shortened and internalized. The invocations are no longer verbalized, but instead they are mentally glossed over—the actual meaning has been deeply ingrained into the Witch's practice. In time, the rite can be performed almost as an immediate series of gestures and internalized expressions. This is how this rite should be performed whenever the Witch is preparing to perform a spirit summoning. The godhead assumption is automatically done after the magic circle is set.

Techniques for Controlling Consciousness, Sensing Spirits, and the Spirit World

We have already covered the basic components of the discipline for meditation and trance, and these practices will be a regular part of your overall practice. Besides equipping you for the godhead assumption rite they will also assist you in learning to sense and perceive the Spirit World. This is a very important achievement and unless you have a natural talent for clairvoyance or clairaudience it will be difficult but not impossible to activate your psychic sensibilities. However, practice will over time make anyone capable of sensing the other world and perceiving spirits in some manner.

A key point to learning how to sense spirits and perceive the Spirit World is to see without looking, hear without listening, and feel without touching. This might sound like a paradoxical or even impossible state, and in some ways it is; but the point is that a Witch must learn to rely on non-physical sense organs—the eyes, ears, and hands of Spirit. If you want to learn to see spirits then you need to either wear a blindfold or close your eyes to slits so they only allow in a limited amount of light. The same is true for hearing spirits, so it becomes important to block out the distractions of physical sound. To feel and sense the presence of spirits you must block out or diminish all other physical senses in order to feel their subtle presence. I know that this sounds counter intuitive, but the very best tool that anyone could possess to learn and fully experience the spirit world would be an isolation tank filled with salt water and kept at body temperature. Most people don't either possess or have access to such a device, so simpler methods must be used instead.

What I would recommend is that during deep trance states you should start wearing a comfortable blindfold and earplugs and attempt to sense and focus on the domain of spirits without the distraction of sight and sound. Most people who undergo this kind of sensory deprivation will experience various kinds of phenomena at first and these should be ignored as distractions. Everyone has differently attuned senses and their ability to perceive spirit typically functions in different ways, so what this experiment will achieve will be unique to each person. Random hallucinations and chaotic visual effects and sounds will occur until something tangible and consistent becomes apparent to your senses; over time as this experiment is repeated—and it should be repeated—this ability will fully manifest.

At the end of this work you will be able to see and hear spirits in some manner, although it will typically be subtle and undramatic. I regret to report that there won't be any Hollywood type special effects to be seen or heard when this faculty is fully activated unless one resorts to hallucinogenic drugs, which I don't recommend. Most of the time when I am sensing spirits or the topology of the spirit world it seems to be almost at the very edge of my perceptions. It is only when I enter into a visionary trance state or engage in dream incubation[25] or waking dreams that I can see things that are vivid and physically real. However, once this ability fully manifests then you can dispense with using a blindfold and earplugs, having now acquired the ability to focus your senses so that distractions are ignored and the subtle perceptions of spirit are amplified.

Spirit vision and hearing are always a kind of barely perceptible phenomena, where the images of spirits and the features of the Spirit World

---

25 Dream incubation is a fancy way of saying sleeping in a temple space in order to receive prophetic dreams from the Spirit World. This is a practice that has its roots in antiquity.

seem to be superimposed over the normal physical senses and the world it perceives.

Keep in mind that what we perceive in the physical world is an interpretation of nerve impulses produced by what our senses are actually detecting. We don't see, hear, smell, taste, or feel what our sensory organs are actually detecting—everything is interpreted in our heads. So, for this reason what we might sense in the spirit world is nothing more than an extension of that interpretation process based on the heightened senses as produced by meditation and trance states.

When you learn how to control self-induced trance states, you will discover that there are various levels of trance that you can experience, from a mild trance state to one that is deep and nearly unconscious. It is in deep trance that the spirit world becomes fully perceptible and realistic, but to acquire this level of immersion requires you to be more unconscious than awake. In such a state of deep trance, you won't be able to perform any ritual actions or physically move about because you won't be conscious of the external world. There is an important balance between how immersed you wish to be within the spirit world or how conscious you need to be of the external world in order to either communicate with others or perform ritual actions.

Once you have developed this ability to see impressions and outlines of the spirit world and engage with spirits in your immediate temple area, you should then expand your work and begin to map out the domain of spirit as it occurs in your local area. Take walking tours of your neighborhood and use your "sight" to reveal the topology of the spirit world around you. I would recommend you do this during the later evening hours when there is less noise and fewer distractions.

Whether you live in the countryside, suburbs, or in an urban setting, you will begin to discover another world that coexists with the one that you have been living in and taking for granted your whole life. You will likely see lines of force representing the spirit corridors (sometimes called "ghost roads") that will be either very crooked or convoluted if you are in the countryside, or mostly straight and Euclidean if you are in an urban area. You will also likely notice topological features, such as trees, hills, rivers, lakes, streams, unique buildings, or wide traffic ways that will also register as features of the spirit world. It is also possible that you will see individual spirits and also groups or clusters of spirits residing at these unique features. A great, large tree might have a whole community of spirits residing in it functioning as a unified entity (a hive mind), or there might be a local deity with its constellation of servitors in that tree. You should investigate your local area and note down everything that you see and experience to build up a useful representation of the domain of spirit in your specific area.

You will also become aware of local deities residing near your home, and it would be prudent to attempt to communicate with them. Knowing the local deities is an important task for a conjuring Witch to accomplish since it will help her to establish her home ground or turf. The most important thing for anyone doing these kinds of activities is to get the names of any spirits or deities encountered. You can also take a sample from that special place where the local deity resides, such as a leaf, acorn, twig, or pebble, and reverently place it in your shrine in order to establish a connection between the local deity and yourself. Another thing that you can do is to surreptitiously leave discrete offerings to the local deity as a way of establishing a tight relationship with it. After a period of time, you will have built up a number of spirit connections and local deity alignments that will greatly add to your own magical presence in your neighborhood.

All this can be accomplished without even performing any kind of spirit summoning. Still, this is the required first step that will take you into the spirit world and greatly enhance your abilities to engage with it and the various entities that reside there. Once you begin to formally summon these various local entities, you will then begin to collect powerful spiritual allies that will join together with you to form a local area network of intelligence and spiritual alliances. Some Witches will find that this achievement will suffice for their conjuring objectives, others will seek to encounter and engage with more advanced entities such as celestial spirits, greater deities, and even angels and demons. The potential for discovery, personal empowerment, and mastery are nearly limitless and each conjuring Witch will take a pathway that is uniquely her own.

Since you are going to be performing deep trance sessions and fully immersing yourself in the domain of spirit or fully assuming your personal godhead, you are also going to need to know how to ground yourself afterward. While I would assume that you would know how to perform this kind of operation, I'll briefly cover it here just to make certain you know exactly what I am talking about.

When exposed to the paranormal realities, influences, and energies of deities, spirits, or magic, it is important to know that you must ground yourself when the working is complete. I have experienced all too many occasions when Witches, Pagans, and even some Ceremonial Magicians have been highly exposed to magical and spiritual influences and then went about afterward as if they were drunk, emotionally unhinged, or even hysterical. A simple grounding exercise is all you need to properly decompress after a potent magical working.

- Stand up fully erect with arms straight out to form a T shape.

- Breathe normally and fully in a completely relaxed manner, and then bring your hands slowly together with the palms touching before your chest.

- Imagine the energy in your body traveling from the head and shoulders, centering in the heart, and then down to the feet.

- Bend down forward and use your hands to direct the energy down through your thighs to the feet and below.

- Crouch down with your hands placed firmly before you on the floor, and gently force the energy in your body out so that it drains completely into the floor.

Other techniques that you can use for grounding include eating, drinking, splashing cold water on your face, or doing something completely mundane, like dancing or even having sex. Sometimes you can go outdoors and put your feet and hands into the earth—that always works, too.

Another important practical technique is centering (known as the Middle Pillar exercise in the Golden Dawn), and there are two techniques for centering. These have already been covered in the previous ritual for godhead assumption, but I will also put them here so they can become an independent part of your practical controlling consciousness repertoire.

Ascending Wave Centering: Celebrant stands in the center of the magic circle with arms down at the sides and performs a centering exercise—imagining seeing a bluish energy focused and moving up the special body points from foot, knee, groin, breast, to crown in an ascending projection. While this is done, the breath is drawn up into the body, held, and then exhaled gently through pursed lips while the celebrant holds her arms above her head, allowing the fingers of her hands to shake and vibrate.

Descending Wave Centering: Celebrant stands in the center of the magic circle with arms down at the sides and performs a centering exercise—imagining seeing a bluish energy focused and moving down the special body points from the crown, breast, groin, knee, to the foot in a descending projection. While this is done, the breath is drawn up into the body, held, and then exhaled gently through pursed lips while the celebrant holds her arms above her head, allowing the fingers of her hands to shake and vibrate.

Centering can be used to help stabilize your bodily and emotional energies with an emphasis on either what is above (opening self) or below (grounding self). You can perform either of these operations without disturbing the energy level or mindset that you have already established through a magical working, unlike an actual grounding.

Building the Tools of the Modern Conjuring Witch: Part Two

We become what we behold. We shape our
tools, and thereafter, our tools shape us.

MARSHALL MCLUHAN

Now that we have covered the first two of the four basic tools, we can continue on with our discussion of the second set. The second set consists of developing spirit characterizations, hierarchies, and defining the nature and use of the symbolic link. We will also examine the preparations one must undergo in order to be ready and fully capable of performing high ritual magic, which might be a new topic for some of you. Let me briefly define what these tools are and then we can examine them in greater detail.

Developing Spirit Characterizations, Hierarchies, and the Symbolic Link—This is the central activity a conjuring Witch performs in order to summon a spirit. She must perform a fair amount of research in order to identify the associated name and all of its characteristics, including its place in a hierarchy of spirits as well as other associated correspondences. She uses a combination of books, the Internet, and her own powers of divination and intuition to determine the nature of the target spirit. There are a number of techniques the Witch can use to derive the characteristics of the spirit; in order to facilitate this research she can begin to engage and subtly contact that spirit while she is making these determinations.

She will also make a sigil from the name of the spirit on some special material such as parchment, for example. If by chance she doesn't possess an already published magical character for this spirit then she will have to create one using a traditional mechanism for deriving sigils. Once she crafts and then consecrates the sigil or character of the spirit, she will have access to that entity, and she can fill in all of the other characteristics research has failed to provide. As far as preparatory work is concerned, it is one of the most important tasks, since it will be performed whenever the Witch seeks to conjure a spirit. I will be quite thorough in showing how to do his task so you can perform this step with complete confidence.

Preparations for High Ritual Magic—When a Witch is developing her rituals and spells to summon a spirit, she will carefully write and assemble all the rituals, including the invocation or evocation liturgy, and then choose a suitable date for the first working. I will go over all of the rituals needed, including the spirit invocations, in enough detail that you will be able to write your own rituals. You will need to practice until you are competent and comfortable with them. You will also need to gather any of the other materials needed. Great care should be exercised in selecting whether to perform an invocation or an evocation. Also, an auspicious date should be selected when such an operation can be performed without interruption. Everything must be in its place and ready for the appointed time; the Witch should be bathed, anointed, and wearing clean vestments. All of these many details will be covered so that nothing is left to chance.

These are the important preliminary steps a conjuring Witch performs in order to prepare for the summoning of a spirit. The first time you will tackle these four steps, there will be a lot of ancillary tasks to complete because you won't have the developed lore or experience to more quickly and efficiently complete them. That will happen later after you have done this operation a few times. You will have to write the rituals and also perform them a number of times before they become easy and familiar to you, and they must be easy and familiar before you attempt to perform an actual spirit summoning.

So what I am proposing is that you experiment with the various practices and rituals you develop in these four steps (found in this and the previous chapter) before you are ready to perform the first conjuring. Take your time to build up the lore and practices. Enjoy all of the crafting and writing, and by all means, gain the necessary confidence that you will need to perform a successful working. There's no hurry and you aren't competing with anyone. As the Wicked Witch of the West so notably said in the movie *Wizard of Oz:* "These things must be done delicately."

Developing Spirit Characterizations, Hierarchies, and the Symbolic Link

As I have said previously, if you want to summon a spirit you have to at least know its name. However, that is only the first of several steps required. The most important product that this preparatory process creates is the symbolic character, seal, or sigil link that is used to establish the symbolized name or mark of a spirit, thus uniquely identifying it. This sigil or character is drawn upon a piece of parchment or other material and then it is consecrated and fully identified as the symbolic representation of the name and character of the target spirit.

In this section we will go over all of the steps that you should follow to prepare yourself for identifying and summoning a spirit into some recognizable manifestation. Since the ability to sense and perceive spirits will vary between conjuring Witches, what occurs when a spirit is summoned will likely differ depending on that ability to see and hear spiritual phenomena.

However, the background to all of this activity consists of one of the most important questions that a Witch should ask, which forms the basic justification for performing the spirit summoning in the first place. That question is namely, "What spirit should be called and why should it be summoned?" Other corollary questions would be: "What is the purpose for summoning that spirit? What do you expect that spirit to do for you, and what are you willing to offer it as a form of compensation? Can the spirit be expected to perform the task that you want it to do?" An even more fundamental question would be, "Is it even possible for the task to be successfully completed by any means?" Asking a spirit to do something that is either impossible or just barely probable is in fact setting up the operation to fail. So, too, is asking a spirit to attempt something that it is not equipped to perform. So there are two things that need to be determined. Is the objective feasible for a spirit to complete, and is the spirit itself capable of achieving a successful outcome?

The best approach to answering these questions is fully understanding what you want to accomplish with a spirit summoning. That means performing some extensive divination and also some deeply internalized concentration exercises on the question. You should know and intimately understand what you want to accomplish and how you want to accomplish it before summoning a spirit and giving it the task. Then you have to determine if the spirit in question is even capable of such a task.

Still, a magical objective that is lacking in clarity, insight, and understanding will produce either a complete failure or it will cause something undesirable or unpleasant to happen instead. You might actually get what you were asking for; but the cost might be very high or the after effects (what we call blowback) might even nullify the objective. Another important consideration is to make certain that what you are asking for is fully justified according to your own sense of ethics and morality. Attempting to do something that you know in your heart is wrong will likely produce results that are disastrous. Clarity and certainty ensures that an operation will be successful and produce the desired results, and only the results, that the conjuring Witch is seeking. One last point is that you should keep your objective simple, therefore making it easy to measure a successful outcome.

However, determining the functional capability of a spirit requires developing a meaningful context for that spirit (such as a category and hierarchy) and also defining its personal characteristics. This analysis will also determine if the working should be an invocation or an evocation. The way that a spirit's ability or function is determined is two-fold. You should know where that spirit resides regarding the three domains of the Spirit World and what specific collective or hierarchy that the spirit belongs to, if any. Spirits don't usually exist alone; in fact, in nearly all of the situations that I am familiar, spirits belong to collective groups, some of which constellate around a demi-god or deity to form a hierarchy. If the target spirit has been taken from a list of spirits found in popular folklore or one of the old grimoires, then some of the attributes associated with that spirit might be used to determine its character. However, nearly all of the descriptions and functions associated with spirits in the old grimoires are problematic at best or completely spurious. Instead, I would like to propose the following methodology for determining the function of a given spirit.

First you should determine where the spirit resides, and this information can be derived from where you have encountered this spirit if it is part of your own research or analysis. The following is a basic common definition of spirit function based on its placement within the three domains of the spirit world.

Celestial spirits: These spirits reside in the highest level and therefore are more remote than all other spirits. They are useful for getting a larger perspective on a given subject than what might be available locally. They are excellent for oracles, prophecies and identifying or promoting long-term processes. They are also inspirational and can assist one in gaining some degree of spiritual ascension, gnosis, and spiritual transformation. Your higher self can readily communicate with these beings and interpret their lofty pronouncements into practical considerations. What these spirits can't do very well is cause material changes or to reveal intimate secrets and mysteries because they are so remote from everyday activities.

Earth-based spirits: These spirits are to be found in and around your local area or neighborhood, and they would particularly include the deities and spirits associated with your homestead. While they might lack the higher-minded sensibilities of celestial spirits, they are much more grounded in the earth, intimately aware of your personal life and therefore much more relevant and practical. They can answer questions about material prospects and situations (jobs, career, health, relationships, wealth, and social situations such as friends, enemies, and family), and they can also influence such matters. They control the bounty of the soil and secure the boundaries of your property and home. They have some powers over life and death, and can foster or aid in all kinds of healing and the ministrations of the life force. (As you can see, these spirits would represent a very important collective for much of the practical magical work that one might wish to accomplish.)

Underworld spirits: These spirits are below the earth and are typically involved with attributes of death, hidden treasures, secrets, social intrigues, the breaking or bending of laws and conventions, and the accomplishment of underhanded or dark deeds. Divination through the spirits of ancestors or the dead (necromancy), the settling of haunting spirits or ghosts and the acquiring of hidden, arcane, or occult knowledge are accomplished through the summoning of spirits of the underworld. The whole of the mysteries of death and rebirth are to be found in the purview of the spirits of the underworld.

These spirits can also assist a person to get untangled from legal difficulties as well as accomplish unlawful deeds without consequences. However, there are also risks in engaging with spirits of the underworld since they might be just as inclined to cause trickery or harm to the Witch summoning them as they are in doing her bidding. This is where hostile and inimical spirits can be found, and it is where dreadful and uncontrollable spirits or even monsters reside. Some of the really bad or malicious spirits that reside here don't have specific names or else that name is very obscure or relatively unknown, so summoning such a spirit might be difficult. However, there are plenty of devils and infernal spirits named in folklore and the old grimoires, so there is still quite a lot of material available for the erstwhile conjuring Witch who has a flare for the dark side.

As you can see, the most useful spirits are those of the earth and below its surface, while the spirits of the celestial spheres and the sky are more remote and not very practical in terms of material objectives. The one exception is the Witch's familiar spirit or Higher Self. Her God/dess Within as spirit intermediary will be able to bridge the gap between the highest and lowest spirits in the various collectives and hierarchies. She should always listen to the advice and guidance of her familiar spirit in order to safely and effectively walk the paths of the Spirit World and engage with spirits to help her perform her magical works. It is also important to never perform any magical working or conjuration for a purpose that goes against the sanctions and boundaries established by the familiar spirit. Pursuing such a foolish course will cause the Witch to lose contact with her familiar spirit for a short period of time; but it might also ensure that the working in question will become an unmitigated disaster. Cleaning up such a mess will take time, and the Witch will have to make amends with her familiar spirit before the status quo can be re-established.

There are always ethical boundaries that the Witch shouldn't cross, and these boundaries will be established and known by both her and the familiar spirit. Since the familiar spirit is nothing more or less than the personalized deity that resides within one, then going against its ethical framework to achieve an illicit objective represents a profound fall from grace. You would never consider doing something against your own best interests (I hope), and crossing the ethical boundary established by the familiar spirit is tantamount to doing the same thing.

Of the eleven categories of spirits shown previously, only some of them represent entities that might be invoked or evoked for specific magical objectives that would directly impact the material world. These spirits would therefore represent the majority of those that the Witch would summon. The following paragraphs represent classification lists of spirits that I would recommend as the most useful.

Celestial intermediaries (3)—These would include angels and demons[26] that act as specific intermediaries or messengers between humans and the deities. If you want to engage a deity to perform a mundane task, then these spirits would be ideal. The thing to remember is that deities

---

26 *Demon* is from the Greek word "daimon" which means intermediary. Later its meaning was altered along with the spelling, to the Latin word *demon*. I would not necessarily include goetic demons as intermediaries unless one is referring to either chthonic deities or infernal princes/chiefs.

deal with macrocosmic schemes, so what is requested would have to be something large and long in duration. The best use of such spirits is to gain some kind of prophetic insight, visionary revelation, or oracular pronouncement. Intermediaries can bestow blessings directly from the deities or carry the essence of sacrifices or votive offerings directly to the gods for some material end.

Sky spirits, such as various storm spirits (5)—These are useful if you have a knack for weather magic. Their attributes include aerial prognostication and to a lesser extent, weather generation.

Winged or aerial spirits (6)—These function as lesser intermediaries between the deities and humanity. They are capable of impacting the material plane, but typically function more as a kind of informant.

Great ancestors, heroes, and masters (7)—These intermediaries function nearly as demigods and are often approached as idealized lineage masters or sources of the greater human heritage. In most cases, they function as the disembodied teachers and guides to humanity, so they are often friendly and benign.

Of course, having a great hero or master fully engaged and on one's side is an object worthy of any magical feat. However, not all great ancestors are open to being summoned in this manner, particularly those who were against any form of magic while alive, such as the spirit of the patriarch Samuel evoked by the Witch of En-dor.[27]

Lesser earth deities and spirits of locality or place (8)—We have already discussed these spirits when defining the use and function of earth-based

---

27 I would also add a number of Catholic and Orthodox saints, and also other cultural intermediaries dedicated to a religious faith exclusive of magic.

spirits. The Fairy folk[28] as well as other mythic earth spirits and creatures would be part of this category. All lawful things of the material plane would be under the control of these spirits.

Underworld and chthonic deities and spirits (9)—Since all deities have chthonic roots, all deities will be found in some form or another in the underworld. Ironically, engaging with a chthonic aspect of a deity could actually be more enrichening and empowering than engaging with its celestial version, although it would be considered more capricious and unpredictable. There are also dark counterparts to all of the earth-based or celestial spirits to be found in the underworld. While the spirits of the underworld vary considerably from each other, their overall area of magical capability is pretty much the same throughout this domain. You would invoke these spirits to achieve unsanctioned or unlawful objectives, and you would also engage them to discover hidden things, secrets or occult knowledge. They also represent raw power that can be used to make things happen in the material world, but all such powers come with cautionary obligations and liabilities.

Determining the hierarchy, sodality, or residence of a spirit can be divined in a number of ways. Perhaps the best way to know as much as possible about the spirit that you want to summon is to informally access it through the artifice of crafting the sigil or symbolic character of the spirit and consecrating it. Once you have a consecrated sigil acting as the sym-

---

28   The Fairy folk also reside in the underworld as well, so knowing the difference would be very important in terms of assessing their capabilities and overall disposition. This was well attested to in the fictional story "Johnathon Strange and Mr. Norell" where the magician Norell summoned a Fairy King (the Gentleman with the Thistledown hair) to resurrect a recently deceased young lady. Such a fairy spirit would have been functionally one residing in the underworld, and the characteristics of his residence, *Kingdom of Lost Hope*, would certainly make this true.

bolic link to that spirit then all you have to do to access it is to take that sigil and enter into a light trance state and seek to communicate with it. You do this by internally calling out its name while holding the sigil before you and staring at it. After a time, you will sense the presence of the spirit and you can then engage with it and retrieve whatever information you need in order to more effectively summon it in a formal manner.

Once you have identified the class (familiar grouping) or category (location) of a spirit, then you can check your various sources of information to build up a standard character or persona of that spirit.[29] For known spirits taken from spirit lists in the old grimoires, you can extend your research to include other sources of information. One of the best resources in my opinion is Davidson's *A Dictionary of Angels*, although it is more comprehensive than the title would indicate. You can also examine the various tables of correspondences in the book *The Complete Magician's Tables* by Stephen Skinner and see if your target spirit is listed in one of the tables. If you are seeking to evoke a demon then *The Dictionary of Demons* written by Michelle Belanger would be useful. You can then compare that entry in the book to other similar entries (in other sources) to get other corresponding attributes for that spirit. All of this information is collected together in your notebook for that specific spirit, including its symbolic character or sigil. Still, the most relevant information is what you can get from the spirit directly through an informal summoning. Also, gaps in your information can be filled in by asking questions and seeking guidance from your familiar spirit.

One simple way to determine the character of the spirit is to examine its name. A name says a lot about that which it names, and this is true about people and also spirits. If you can determine the language that the name is derived from then you might be able determine the meaning of that name

---

29   A class of spirits is its familiar grouping, such as archangels, goetic demons, fairies, earth elementals, etc.

and also something about the character of the spirit. A simple way to discover the meaning and attribute associated with the name (particularly if you don't have an interest in linguistics) is to convert it to a Hebrew spelling. This is done by using the Hebrew alphabet to convert most of the consonants and some of the vowels from the English alphabet spelling. You can use a creative approach to perform this derived Hebrew spelling. Once you have completed this task, you will exchange each translated letter for one of the trump cards in the major arcana of the tarot and read the sequence of cards like a linear tarot card reading. I have used this method many times to extract the occult significance of a name that would otherwise be untranslatable and unintelligible.

- **Example:** Spirit Name—Vassago—**Hebrew:** VShAGV [30]—
  Tarot Trumps: Hierophant—Aion (Last Judgement)—
  Fool—Priestess—Hierophant (final). **Reading:** Spiritual
  mastery—awakening—internalization (freedom)—divine
  intervention—personal empowerment. (It would seem
  that Vassago has quite a few celestial capabilities even
  though he resides in the underworld as a goetic demon—
  best of both worlds!)

Still, crafting the sigil or symbolic character is the most important preparation task that you will perform before performing an invocation or evocation. There are a number of ways of doing this and we should cover the basic set that you would use to produce a consecrated sigil symbolizing the name of the spirit. A name and a consecrated symbol are

---

30 This is the Hebrew spelling according to Crowley's book of tables in *Liber 777*.
You could also use different spellings as well to get a different set of Hebrew
letters. Notice that the first letter *a* has been omitted and that the double *s* is
actually the letter *shin* or *sh*. This is a typical rendition of an English, Latin,
or Greek name into the Hebrew alphabetic spelling. Not all vowels are
retained, but use your best creative approximation.

all that you need to either invoke or evoke a spirit. The sigil or symbolic character as rendered on a piece of consecrated parchment or other material is the magical link needed to identify that spirit within the Spirit World. Let us discuss how this important device is derived, inscribed and blessed with the four elements and spirit so that it is consecrated.

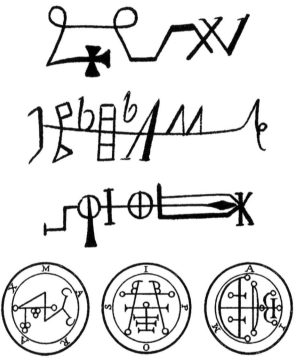

Figure 10: diagram of a few examples of angels and sigils from the old grimoires (top to bottom, left to right: Michael, Gabriel, Raphael, Marax, Ipos, and Aim)

First of all, if you have selected this spirit from amongst the known spirits in a source, such as one of the classic old grimoires, then the spirit will likely have some kind of symbolic character or seal already derived for that spirit. This is true for many of the spirits in the *Lemegeton* (*Lesser Key of Solomon*) or the *Grimoirum Verum* (*True Grimoire*).

However, in most cases you will only possess a spirit's name so there won't be an already derived symbolic character for the spirit. You will have to create one, and this symbolic mark is called a sigil.

There are a few different ways to craft a sigil, but the first thing that you will have to do is determine the exact spelling of the spirit's name and also what alphabet would be used to write it.

There are several basic techniques for designing a sigil. We will be focusing on just one, the simplest method. The method that I am proposing uses an alphabet wheel.

A sigil is produced by tracing the connecting lines between each of the letters in the name on the wheel. There are three different wheels, so this is where knowing the alphabet used for the spirit's name is an important factor in choosing the correct wheel.

These three alphabet wheels are identically composed of three concentric rings that divide the target alphabet into three groups. They are constructed for the Hebrew, Greek, and English (Latin) alphabets.

Figuring out which wheel to use is important, but it is also relatively easy to determine. If you are trying to create a sigil based on a name that you have discovered yourself that is not part of any tradition then I would recommend using the English alphabet wheel.

If, on the other hand, you are dealing with a spirit that has a historical reference then you can determine if it is ether Hebrew or Greek. Angel names ending in -EL or -YH are Hebrew, so you would use the Hebrew alphabet wheel to construct a sigil for that spirit.

Many names of demons such as the famous goetic demons would incorporate either the Greek alphabet or English (Latin) alphabet wheel. You could also try the Hebrew alphabet wheel if the name was obviously from the Old Testament or from Qabalistic sources.

One thing to keep in mind is the crafting of sigils is an artistic endeavor. There isn't a right or wrong way to design one as long as all of the letters are represented in the sigil. The important thing is to be consistent.

If you develop a certain methodology that works for you then you should use it in the same manner for all of your sigil crafting. What I have found is that different practitioners have their own ways of crafting sigils, and one magician might find a different way of doing it than another.

They might produce unique results where their sigils would look somewhat different, but it doesn't matter. Each sigil, if crafted in a consistent manner and properly consecrated, will perform as intended. The important point is that the sigil symbolically represents the name of the spirit, and that intention formulated by the Witch, however it is executed, is the defining one.

Once you have selected the alphabet ring you want to use, you will place some tracing paper over it and then starting with the first letter of the name, draw a line from that cell in the wheel to the next letter in the wheel using a straight edge.

You will repeat this step for each of the letters until you have drawn a sigil consisting of a continuous line connecting all the letters spelled in the spirit's name.

Repeating letters grouped together can be notated with a slight curling loop or a zigzag kept within the cell belonging to that letter. You can identify the first letter of the sigil with a serif, circle, or cross, and the final letter with an arrow.

Once you have completed tracing the sigil, you can transfer it to the piece of parchment using ink. You could also carefully draw and then etch it on metal or ceramic, or even burn it on wood.

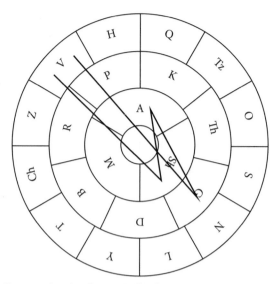

Figure 11: diagram showing how a sigil is drawn on an alphabet wheel (step 1)

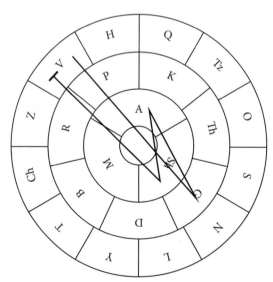

Figure 12: diagram showing how a sigil is drawn on an alphabet wheel (step 2)

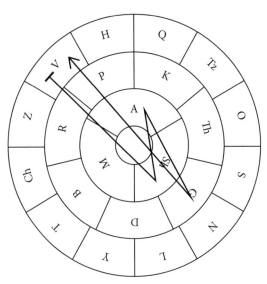

Figure 13: diagram showing how a sigil is drawn on an alphabet wheel (step 3)

In the example above I have shown the three basic steps used in crafting a sigil of the goetic demon Vassago (Hebrew: VShAGV) with the Hebrew alphabet wheel. These three steps are:

1. Draw the lines connecting the five letters V-Sh-A-G-V.

2. Draw a serif cross on the line at the beginning of the line to show the first letter.

3. Draw an arrow on the line at the end to show the final letter. The final linear form is the sigil that one could use for Vassago. However, Vassago also has a traditionally associated seal in the grimoire called the *Goetia* (first book of the *Lemegeton*, or *Lesser Key of Solomon*), and this would be typically used instead.

Figure 14: diagram showing the magical seal of Vassago from the grimoire Goetia

Consecrating the sigil is done in the magic circle using only incense if it is parchment, and additionally "lustral" water (consecrated salt water), oil, and a touch of candle flame if it is metal, ceramic, or wood. You can also either touch it with the point of your athamé (projecting the power into it) or laying the blade upon it for a period of time. You can make up any kind of declaration used at that point, such as: *"I consecrate this sacred sigil of the spirit N in the names of [god-name] and [god-name]. So mote it be."* Then you should just hold the sigil in your hand and focus your gaze upon it, saying in your mind, "You are the Spirit N." You should then wrap up the sigil in a dark cloth and place it on your altar or shrine until you intend on using it for either an informal or a formal summoning. I would further recommend you make this a deeply solemn but simple rite.

Figures 15, 16, and 17 show examples of the three alphabet circles that you can use to build sigils.

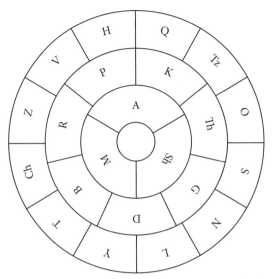

Figure 15: diagram of the Hebrew Alphabet Wheel

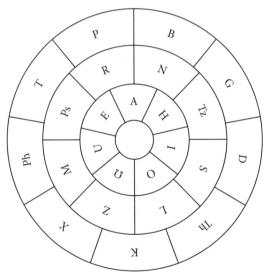

Figure 16: diagram of the Greek Alphabet Wheel

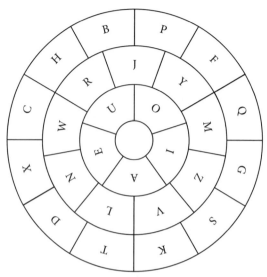

Figure 17: diagram of the English/Latin Alphabet Wheel

When looking at these three wheels, you should notice that the three rings of each contain a varied number of cells or divisions with a single letter occupying that area. Each alphabet is divided into three groups and the rationale for these groups are explained in the following text. The Hebrew alphabet wheel is associated with the three letter groups of the three mothers and the seven double and twelve single letters. This is a culturally determined division for these letters and it is a normal feature of the writing system of the Hebrew language. Thus the Hebrew alphabet wheel has three cells in the inner ring, seven in the middle, and twelve in the outer ring.

The Greek Alphabet wheel is also divided into three groups; but this grouping is more linguistically based. It is divided into seven vowels, eight semi-vowels, and nine voiceless consonants for a total of twenty-four letters. The inner, middle, and outer rings have the number of cells with the appropriate letters placed in them for each of these three groups.

The English alphabet wheel is divided into three groups consisting of five vowels, nine voiced consonants, and twelve voiceless consonants for a total of twenty-six letters. Latin has a similar configuration since there are also five vowels, but there are only seventeen consonants for a total of twenty-two letters. You can use the English wheel to build a sigil from a Latin name just using those letters that are associated with the Latin alphabet.

Ceremony of Naming and Un-naming

Perhaps the simplest of all spells associated with spirit conjuration uses what I call the ceremony of naming and un-naming. This is a simple spell that is used to *informally* contact a spirit prior to performing an actual formal evocation.

As previously stated, an informal contact or summoning is one that doesn't constrain and bind the spirit. This spell can be used on any spirit where the name is known, but the qualities of the spirit are unknown. Like any magical rite, it is performed in a consecrated magic circle.[31]

The ceremony of naming uses the letters of the spirit's name to build up or reduce it incrementally from the right to the left or left to the right, respectively, until the full name is expressed or one letter is expressed. It begins with a single letter and joins to it the next letter in the name, then the next, and so on. Conversely, it can also reduce the full name letter by letter until only one remains.

Here's an example.

---

31   This rite is used to determine the nature of spirits that are not considered deities, demigods, great ancestors, or any other spirit that would be obviously invoked instead of evoked.

Ceremony of Naming for the spirit Nogorathes [32]

S
ES
HES
THES
ATHES
RATHES
ORATHES
GORATHES
OGORATHES
NOGORATHES

Ceremony of Un-naming for the spirit Nogorathes

NOGORATHES
OGORATHES
GORATHES
ORATHES
RATHES
ATHES
THES
HES
ES
S

As previously stated, the Witch conjurer can use the ceremony of naming and un-naming to informally summon a spirit and also dismiss or release it. It is an antique method and a really good one. I still use it myself, although I usually add to it other summoning techniques.

---

32 There is no spirit in my workings named Nogorathes—I decided to use this name because it doesn't refer to any spirit and therefore, is not active.

You can slowly and sonorously intone each iteration of the spirit's name and either build up or redact it, and you can do this once or three times depending on your inclination. When attempting to determine the nature and character of a spirit prior to formally summoning it, you can use this simple rite to engage a spirit and establish the beginnings of a relationship with it.

You should perform this rite within a consecrated circle, using the consecrated sigil to assist or lend a focused connection to the target spirit. What follows are the recommended steps:

1. Consecrate a magic circle.

2. Sit in the center of the circle with a lit candle and a small stick of burning incense.

3. Hold the consecrated sigil in your hand and stare intently into it.

4. While staring at the sigil, begin the intoning of the name letter by letter, starting with the first letter. Proceed until the name is fully expressed. Do this operation once or three times.

5. Meditate and seek to gain a connection with the target spirit. You can attempt to communicate with it mentally or through the use of a thrown die.

6. Once completed, extinguish the candle and incense and close the circle.

This simple rite can be done as many times as needed so that the conjuring Witch has all of the information required to determine the method and approach for a formal evocation.

To perform the ceremony of un-naming, you would perform the same steps above, but the purpose would be to break any contact, and the name redaction would be performed just once. It might also be prudent to burn the spirit's sigil at the end of the rite. The ceremony of un-naming would be performed to fully and completely banish and break all contact with a spirit. This is rarely done, but sometimes it is prudent to completely disengage from a spirit if you have determined that performing a formal evocation would be either useless (it's the wrong spirit for the job) or hazardous (spirit is too aggressive or inimical to the conjuror). An informal contact is also one that is easy to break if required because it has no obligations.

An interesting side note is that if you look across and then down at this naming or un-naming pattern you will notice that the name is spelled either forward or backward and also across—this could be considered a kind of palindrome that is most effective in magical workings.

Once you have crafted the sigil, performed the required research, consulted your familiar spirit, performed divination, and also completed several informal summoning rites, then you can collect all of this material together and write it into your *Liber Spirituum* or Book of Spirits. The purpose for these operations is that you need to build up as thorough a dossier on the spirit as possible so that it becomes fully realized before you even perform the formal summoning rite. Additionally, you will write up the diary entries for the actual invocation or evocation and also the formal agreement between you and the spirit and the timeframe in which you wish to see the objective completed. Everything that you experience in your encounters with this target spirit should be written up in this book. Later on, it will become the most valuable book in your possession.

Preparations for High Magic

We have covered all of the various parts that you need to know in order to perform a spirit summoning rite. Now it is time to show you how all the components join to formulate a specific set of rituals you will have to research, develop, and write up beforehand. In order to function optimally as a Witch who has graduated to performing the rituals of high or ritual magic, you will need scripts to follow in order to perform the ritual actions and either read from or recite the associated verbal declarations. You can make these rituals elaborate or simple, but when you are starting out, I would recommend you make them simple and succinct. You can always embellish them later on when you have mastered this process.

There are basically two rituals that you will have to write, and these are the Rose Ankh vortex and the Western Gateway rites. You will also need to develop your battery of invocations and the methods for constraining, binding, and releasing the target spirit. The basic outline for the ritual actions consists of the following thirteen steps. The first two steps are based on your own tradition or they can be developed just for this kind of magical working.

1. Circle Consecration rite

2. Raising the Power (Pyramid or Cone)—optional

3. Godhead assumption

4. Establishing the Rose Ankh vortex

5. Opening the Western Gateway

6. Invocation and Summoning

7. Communion—optional (Invocation)

8. Constraining—optional (Evocation)

9. Binding—optional (Evocation)

10. Release

11. Closing the Western Gateway

12. Sealing the Rose Ankh vortex

13. Grounding

When you perform the godhead assumption, you will do it with a light trance state so that you will be able to perform the other rites without any distractions.

You should feel the presence of your personal godhead, but it should be internalized so that it empowers instead of incapacitating you.

When performing the simplified and internalized version of the godhead assumption, you should face the shrine and open yourself to all of the holy relics and statues established there.

Steps 6 through 10 will be covered in detail in the next chapter, so that leaves us to discuss the establishing of the Rose Ankh vortex, opening the Western gateway, and then closing the gateway and sealing the vortex—steps 4 and 5, and 11 and 12. We have already covered how to ground in a previous section.

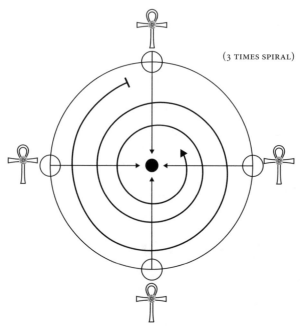

Figure 18: diagram of the Rose Ankh Vortex being erected—with Rose Ankh figures with arrows showing how each is drawn

Establishing the Rose Ankh Vortex

Building or erecting the underworld vortex using the Rose Ankh device is a simple rite with very few steps. You should have already erected the consecrated magic circle and raised power within that structure. The key point to this operation is that it is performed in a widdershins or counterclockwise arc, the opposite of how a consecrated circle is established or a cone of power is raised. Also, instead of setting the four Watchtowers at the cardinal points where they polarize each other at the periphery of the circle, they are instead drawn together into the center of the circle at the nadir. Setting the four Rose Ankhs at the four Watchtowers causes the vortex to become a magnetic-invoking container perfect for summoning spirits.

How you draw the Rose Ankh in the air requires a bit of imagination and visualization. Draw the Rose Ankh in four parts using the wand (arm, looping head of the cross, bottom line or connecting foot, and the invoking spiral in the center). As you draw it, imagine your wand making a line of bluish energy in the air before you. Then when you are drawing the invoking spiral in the center of the Rose Ankh, project your power into the figure while simultaneously exhaling. If you need help visualizing the drawing of the figure in the air, then use a lit stick of incense in a dim or darkened room. This will help you to actually see the figure as you draw it, and then later when you use a wand, it will be something that you can easily imagine. Also, once you draw a Rose Ankh in the air, you should continue to imagine seeing it at the previous place in the circle as you draw the next one. When you are completed, you should visualize a Rose Ankh energetically shining in each of the four watchtowers, connected by a ring of bluish flame.

The same method is used to draw a line from one already established Rose Ankh to the next Watchtower in sequence. Move your wand hand slowly along the periphery of the circle (and lightly exhale) as if you were drawing a line of bluish energy at shoulder height from one Watchtower to the next. When using the sword to join the Rose Ankh to the center of the circle, point it at the device and then draw a line with the sword to the center of the circle at the nadir. This will produce a glowing line of bluish flame slanting down from the Rose Ankh to the floor of the circle at the center point. When you are done drawing all four Rose Ankhs to the nadir of the circle in this manner, you should visualize a magical construct of a ring of four Rose Ankhs within a web of lines connecting them to the center floor of the circle. Then when you perform the widdershins circumambulation from the periphery of the circle to the center, you will visualize the whole magical construct spiraling into the center of the circle and down below the floor, creating a vortex. The vortex will powerfully draw everything into it, but the magic circle (set previously) will resist being pulled into the center and maintain the integrity of the overall structure. The stress created by this polarization generates the energy of the Rose Ankh vortex.

Here is the outline for the ritual with comments to assist you in writing up your own version. The theme for this ritual should be something having to do with four female deities, such as the maiden, lover, mother, and crone symbology of some traditions of Witchcraft. The ritual cycle begins in the north and ends in the east. This is the opposite of how a circle is consecrated, which is set starting in the east and ending in the north.

1. Proceed to the Northern Watchtower and draw a Rose Ankh in the air with the hand or a wand. Project into the device an imagined violet colored light using the hand or wand and then recite or read a declaration whose theme is the Goddess as Crone.

2. Draw a line from the Rose Ankh in the north and proceed to the western Watchtower and draw a Rose Ankh in the air.

Project into the device an imagined violet-colored light and then recite or read a declaration whose theme is the Goddess as Mother.

3. Draw a line from the Rose Ankh in the west and proceed to the southern Watchtower and draw a Rose Ankh in the air. Project into the device an imagined violet-colored light and then recite or read a declaration whose theme is the Goddess as Lover.

4. Draw a line from the Rose Ankh in the south and proceed to the eastern Watchtower and draw a Rose Ankh in the air. Project into the device an imagined violet-colored light and then recite or read a declaration whose theme is the Goddess as Maiden. Draw a line from the Rose Ankh in the south to the device in the north. (Put down the wand if it has been used.)

5. Take the sword or athamé and stand in front of the northern watchtower and the device (Rose Ankh) and then draw it in a straight line to the center of the circle to the nadir (floor).

6. With the sword or athamé, stand in front of the western Watchtower and the device and then draw it in a straight line to the center of the circle to the nadir (floor).

7. With the sword or athamé, stand in front of the southern Watchtower and the device and then draw it in a straight line to the center of the circle to the nadir (floor).

8. With the sword or athamé, stand in front of the eastern Watchtower and the device and then draw it in a straight line to the center of the circle to the nadir (floor). Then put the sword or athamé in its resting place.

9. Starting in the north at the outer periphery of the circle, circumambulate around the circle three times so that each

circuit draws closer to the center of the circle, which is where you should end. (You can recite a simple repetitive poem while performing this circumambulation.)

10. Kneel before the center of the circle and with your hands, project the power of the energy field into the floor and below.

Sealing the Rose Ankh Vortex

Sealing the five points of the vortex is accomplished using what is called a sealing spiral. A sealing spiral is drawn with a widdershins or counter clockwise spiral traveling from the outer periphery to the center in one circuit. This can be done with the hand or a wand.

1. Proceed to the eastern Watchtower and draw a sealing spiral in the air. Imagine that circle point being sealed and frozen when the seal is completed.

2. Proceed to the southern Watchtower and draw a sealing spiral in the air. Imagine that circle point being sealed and frozen when the seal is completed.

3. Proceed to the western Watchtower and draw a sealing spiral in the air. Imagine that circle point being sealed and frozen when the seal is completed.

4. Proceed to the northern Watchtower and draw a sealing spiral in the air. Imagine that circle point being sealed and frozen when the seal is completed.

5. Proceed to the center of the circle and draw to the floor a sealing spiral. Imagine that the whole vortex ritual structure is sealed and frozen now that all five points are sealed.

Opening the Western Gateway

The western gateway ritual structure is based on the triangle as the symbol for a door. The three points of the gate represent the guide, guardian, and the ordeal associated with the passage from one world or level to the next.

In some situations, the guide and guardian can be the same entity, representing the fact that assistance and insight only comes to those who are worthy of making the passage.

Such an entity is a lintel demigod who is the first spirit that one encounters when seeking to enter into the spirit world. A lintel demigod is a deity who wards the gateway between the spirit world and our own world. Often this deity is a lesser deity (demigod) who has the specific role of a gate keeper.

This demigod has many names in many different traditions or cultures: Papa Legba or Exu in the Afro-Caribbean/Brazilian traditions; Hermes, Mercury, Janus, Artemis, Diana, or Hecate Triformis in the Greco-Roman traditions; and the unnamed Dread Lords in traditional Witchcraft. When the Guide and Guardian aspects are joined, the crossroads demigod can also be depicted as a trickster or shapeshifter. In many traditions, the Guardian-Guide appears as an old man (grandfather) or an old woman (grandmother) who can assume the shape of a friendly and helpful person or a terrifying monster. The passage ordeal itself is symbolized by the open jaws of a monster or great serpent, representing that the passage can be frightening and even dangerous.

In building this ritual, you have to find some kind of representation for these three attributes of guide, guardian, and ordeal. When understood in the semantic guise of thesis, antithesis, and synthesis, these three attributes are better grasped and understood in the context of this ritual. The focus of the ritual will assume that the celebrant is standing in the east and facing the west. On her left hand (southeast) will be the guide (the operator's weakest point), to her right hand (northeast) will be the guardian (her strongest point), and in front of her will be the ordeal of the gateway passage. Thus the guide will protect the operator's weakest side, the guardian will challenge the operator at her side of greatest strength, and the ordeal will be before her (and not behind her). Since this is the gateway that leads "down" into the spirit world as a form of "underworld passage," then the theme will have to be designed as depicting a descent into a world of darkness and night, even though the Spirit World does have three levels overall. The operator will imagine a descent below the level of the floor of the magic circle where the underworld resides.

As the ultimate designer of this ritual, you will have to research the concept of lintel gods or spirits as they are represented in your tradition and either keep the guardian and guide distinct or join them into one being with two aspects. You can also choose specific deities or spirits from any tradition that appeals to you, or consult with your familiar spirit and discover the names and natures of these spirits as they pertain to your personal spiritual path. Even if you fail to come up with a name or names, as long as you declare the nature and character of these entities within your ritual then you will have provided enough detail to write up and perform this ritual. You will perform this ritual every time you work any kind of summoning rite, so over time it will evolve and likely change, and the details will become much clearer after you have undergone a few experiments.

The following is the outline you should use to develop and write this ritual.

1. Stand in the east facing the western Watchtower. Extend your arms out to reach to the southeast and northeast angles. Declare your intention to make a passage into the spirit world by the power and wisdom of the guardian and the guide.

2. Turn to the southeast and draw at that point in the circle an invoking spiral (clockwise spiral from outside periphery to the center) with your hand and then point into the center of the spiral just drawn. Declare and describe the help and assistance of the guide who will render aid to make a successful passage. (You use an invoking spiral to invoke the gateway entity at that point in the circle.)

3. Turn to the northeast and draw at that point in the circle an invoking spiral with your hand and then point into the center of the spiral just drawn. Declare and describe the barriers and tests that the guardian will use to ensure that one is worthy to make the passage.

4. Face the west and draw at that point in the circle an invoking spiral with your hand and then point into the center of the spiral just drawn. Declare the nature of the ordeal that one must undergo in order to achieve the passage. The ordeal is always a variation of the same story: to undergo a shattering and breakup of the self and then to experience the self as reintegrated and reborn in a new form.

5. Draw the three points of the triangular gate together starting in the southeast and proceeding to the west, then the northeast and again in the southeast. You will turn to face each point of the circle, pivoting on your heel as you draw the triangle using a continuous line.

6. Face the west and then proceed to walk slowly toward the western Watchtower, pausing briefly to place the index finger before the lips in the expression of silence, and then continuing on until reaching the Watchtower.

7. Make the opening portal gesture—pretend that you are slowly opening a heavy curtain that lies before you and the Watchtower. Once open, take a single step forward and then turn to face the east. Feel the energy of the gateway shower your head with power and light, and then proceed slowly (down) to the center of the circle.

8. Touch the floor in the center of the circle and declare that you have arrived and successfully made your passage into the spirit world.

Closing the Western Gateway

1. Proceed to stand before the western Watchtower and make the closing portal gesture—pretend that you are slowly closing a heavy curtain that has been opened before you. Your hands should meet before you with a quiet clapping sound. Then draw a sealing spiral (widdershins outside to inside) over the Watchtower—the gateway is closed. (A sealing spiral is used instead of a banishing spiral because you are sealing or freezing that point in the magic circle. Remember, the banishing spiral is not effective in a vortex.)

2. Turn to face the east and walk (upwards) to the eastern Watchtower, then turn again to face the west.

3. Turn to the southeast and draw a sealing spiral (widdershins outside to inside) to the southeast point.

4. Turn to the northeast and draw a sealing spiral (widdershins outside to inside) to the northeast point.

5. Turn again to the west and briefly bow.

Spirit Conjuration
for the Modern Witch

But, soft: behold! Lo where it comes again! I'll cross it,
though it blast me.—Stay, illusion! If thou hast
any sound, or use a voice. Speak to me.

HAMLET 1, 1

Now that we have covered everything that you will need to know
and do in order to either invoke or evoke a spirit, we should cover
the actual steps that you will follow when performing a summoning
type magical working.

As stated previously, an invocation is used to summon a deity, demigod,
great ancestor, or any intermediators who are amicable and friendly.
An evocation is used to summon all of the other spirits that are neutral, aggressive, or even hostile. You will have to make that determination yourself, but I have already presented some basic practical rules to
help you identify where that distinction can be made. Even chthonic

deities, whether aggressive or hostile, are of such an elevated status that attempting to summon them using an evocation would be insulting and possibly produce chaotic or dangerous results. Your chief aid and assistant is always your familiar spirit or higher self, and this personal godhead will help you to make good judgments and treat spirits in a fair and respectful manner.

Probably the most difficult decision you will have to make is which spirit to invoke or evoke first. The world is filled with spirits, and there are so many from which to choose. Yet you should inaugurate your profession of being a conjuring Witch performing your first act of summoning by targeting one of the local spirits in your neighborhood. I am making this recommendation because it would represent the place where you should focus your efforts first and foremost—your own back yard. This also means that you will have to spend some time and effort in mapping out your local area and discovering the spirits and deities that reside there. This is a safe and cautious approach to spirit conjuring; but it is also one that requires a fair amount of psychic investigation instead of researching books and online materials. So, it would not be too easy to successfully complete this task.

In the previous chapter, I went through all of the preparations that you will need to follow in order to get to the point where you could actually invoke or evoke a spirit and experience a successful outcome. Once you have successfully completed all of those tasks and have assembled the rituals and equipment that you need to perform this rite, the next time you go through this process it will require less tasks and take less time. However, it is important to carefully prepare for a conjuration. It doesn't matter if it takes several days or more to prepare because the more time you spend carefully preparing for this working then the better the outcome.

As for determining the target spirit to summon, what to do or expect from such a working, and how to progress through a series of workings and develop a strategy for mastering the art of spirit summoning, I will leave that for the next chapter. We will also get more deeply into how to establish a relationship with various spirits, deities, and demigods in addition to the ones that are identified to your tradition of Witchcraft or Paganism. In this chapter, we will focus on the basic steps to summon a spirit, whether through invocation or evocation. Both methods will be fully covered in this chapter, since they represent the central techniques for calling, summoning, and manifesting a target spirit.

Evocation has five steps and invocation only has three, but they have at least the first two steps in common. These five steps are consecration, invocation, constraining, binding, and releasing. An evocation uses all five of these steps, but the invocation uses the first two plus another step called communion. Since invocation is typically used with deities, demigods, great and honored ancestors or heroes, and exalted intermediaries, there is a potential requirement to make offerings to them and also to share sacraments blessed by their presence.

Additionally, an invocation is also an important stage where the Witch can align herself with the entity, requiring a token associated with this being be installed in the shrine and receive offerings on a semi regular basis. Any entity invoked with the purpose of establishing a permanent bond should be given this degree of respect and veneration over a period of time or for as long as the Witch seeks to use her relationship with this entity as a means to achieving goals or bending events to her will. We will go more deeply into these considerations in the next chapter.

However, for this chapter we will focus on the five steps a Witch will dutifully follow when performing an evocation. I will also describe the method that a communion rite can be performed for an invocation. Let us now go over each of these steps and discuss in detail what each entails and must be done for a successful outcome.

Consecration

The first step is consecration, and what it represents is all the preparation steps required up to the moment the Witch begins to call and summon the spirit through an invocation of some kind. Consecration is where you, your vestments, and the temple have been completely sacralized with magical power and spiritual grace. It is a gradual step-by-step series of tasks that results in a complete preparedness for performing the summoning. Here are the steps that you should take to be ready for the next phase in the evocation process.

First of all, you should have established the foundation of your spiritual and magical discipline. It is something that you are performing periodically and regularly without fail, especially well before you begin to prepare for a magical working. This foundation should consist of the following operations.

1. **Godhead assumption**—This rite is performed regularly according to the phases of the moon. Prior to a working, you should be performing once a week, and then every day for three days before the working.

2. **Meditation and trance sessions**—These should be performed daily. On the day of the working, they should be performed periodically until the time of the working.

3. **Divination sessions**—You need to know about yourself and about the objectives that you want a spirit summoning to help you achieve. This can also help you to determine whether the timing of the operation will be auspicious for a successful outcome. Divination can include tarot, rune stones, astrology, and other mechanisms such as dice or knucklebones.

4. **Ritual practice and memorization**—You don't have to completely memorize the rituals you will use to summon a spirit, but you should be very familiar with them and also comfortable performing them.

Crafting and consecrating the sigil is the next step and probably one of the most important ones. In addition to creating and blessing the sigil, you will also assemble a profile or dossier on the spirit, collecting whatever information can be acquired to fully characterize the spirit.

Once you have produced a consecrated sigil of the target spirit, you can use it to begin informally calling and summoning the spirit. This process of access and engagement will start to prepare you (and the target spirit) for the formal summoning. You can also acquire additional information and make some important judgments about the spirit's character and sentiments before being formally summoned. Information acquired in this manner might even persuade you not to perform a formal summoning. There is no harm in backing out at this point, although you will have opened yourself somewhat to the spirit by creating its sigil and informally calling to it.[33]

Spend some time in your meditation session to ponder over your objectives for this working. Question yourself about why you are performing this task. You need to be absolutely certain that this operation is something that you must perform.

Select a proper day and time for the actual working. Of course, it should be far enough in the future to allow you to fully prepare. I would recommend performing this working on a weekend or during a long weekend holiday or a planned short vacation. You need to make certain that you are completely free of all duties and mundane considerations

---

33 You may have to perform the ceremony of un-naming and then burn the sigil to fully break the connection.

so that nothing will distract you from performing your magical work. Pick a time at night or very early in the morning when there will be fewer people in your neighborhood who will be up and about. As far as the days of the lunar month are concerned, the days from just after the new moon up to preceding a full moon are optimal due to the waxing of the moon. Of course, this will depend on whether the spirit is aligned to the light or darkness, since the time preceding a full moon is full of light (at night), and after the last quarter the night is dark and bereft of light. (We will look at the lunation cycle in the next chapter to help you determine the best lunar day for a working.)

A week before the working, begin to raise the energy in your temple and make daily offerings to the deities in your shrine. Clean the temple area out and also launder your robes and other garments you will be wearing for the working. Make certain that the area for the working will be clean and well ordered. Using the sacraments generated from the communion rites with your personal godhead, hold a piece of consecrated bread and take it around the temple area, projecting its blessings into the area. You can also periodically burn incense and keep votive candles lit for the last three days before the working.

During the last three days before the working you should begin a light fast. Eat simple and modest meals that keep you energized but don't weigh you down with a stomach full of heavy food. Eat less meat, lighter meat products such as fish or chicken, or perhaps even no meat at all. Make certain that you have some already prepared food for the day of the working, especially for the grounding feast that should take place once the working is completed.

On the day of the working, avoid all forms of caffeine or other stimulants. You should be completely rested and ready for the work. Lightly break your fast and spend much of the day doing very light duty and spending much of the time meditating and communing with your personal godhead. Be aware of the time as the day progresses, marking the events of dawn, noon, and sunset. At sunset take a long purification bath, anoint yourself with fragrant oils afterward, and then don your vestments. Continue meditating until the hour of the working.

At the appointed time, perform the following five rituals:

1. Circle Consecration rite
2. Raising the Power (Pyramid or Cone)—optional
3. Godhead assumption
4. Establishing the Rose Ankh vortex
5. Open the Western Gateway

You are now ready for the next phase of the working.

Invocation: Summoning and Calling the Spirit

Invocation is where the Witch calls, summons, and implores the target spirit to appear before her using sacred names and barbarous words of power to back up her exhortations.

This is the specific script that is used to call a spirit whether the rite itself is an evocation or an invocation. The rite of summoning reaches a climax at this point of the working.

Whether the summoning succeeds or fails has more to do with all of the previous steps than it has with the actual wording or verbalization of the invocation script. It helps to have a well-written invocation. It also greatly assists the summoning process if the Witch executes it with a loud and clearly articulated voice along with a few howls, screeches, and ululations for added effect.

The invocation was originally based on the rite of exorcism, where the verbal commands given to an evil spirit to vacate the possessed body of a victim were changed so that it invited the spirit to approach and appear instead of being banished.[34] I refer to invocation scripts as reversed exorcisms, and curiously in the old grimoires the celebrant who summons spirits is called an exorcist.

Essentially, the invocation script has the following formulaic text, and except for the differences in the holy names and words of power used, they are practically uniform.

> *"I summon and call you, spirit N, in the names of... and by the authority of... to come forth and appear in this circle and do my bidding. I say these mighty and sacred words of power to make you appear before me in this very place and time."* *[This is followed with a string of barbarous words of evocation, sometimes quite long, that are nearly shouted or seemingly so.]*

As you can see, the invocation script is nothing more or less than a series of commands made to the spirit so that it will appear before the one performing the conjuration. There are, of course, many elaborations on this verbal pattern, and there can also be more than one invocation.

Some grimoires have a first, second, and even a third invocation, followed by coercive curses and verbal punishment meted out to recalcitrant spirits that fail to appear. As you might guess, we won't be using any of that material; Witches approach all spirits in a respectful and reverential manner. We summon with the power of our will assisted with the aegis of our personal godhead, so there is no need to act superior or hostilely toward the target spirit.

A Witch performs the invocation as a means to put herself into a powerful altered state, so she will likely keen, screech, moan, and perhaps even

---

34 You can also write a banishing declaration that can be used as an exorcism based on the same pattern as an evocation rite. The conjuring Witch has the ultimate power to perform either a summoning or a banishing rite to attract or deflect a spirit.

briefly howl in order to get herself into the proper mental state. Even so, she will not denigrate the target spirit nor treat it as an inferior being because the sole reason for calling it is for the mutual benefit of both. There is an old saying that honey attracts more flies (help) than vinegar—being pleasant will help a person's cause much more than being harsh or sour in disposition.

Two points have to be considered when writing up your own version of an invocation script: in whose name are you commanding this spirit to appear and by whose authority. What power and authority is backing up your declarations to the spirit that it must appear before you? This is more of a concern for those conjurors subscribing to the Abrahamic faiths since they are temporarily borrowing the power and authority of their deity in order to have the gravitas to summon spirits. Since nearly all of the old grimoires were written by and for individuals who practiced magic as members of the Abrahamic faith, invocation scripts have this pattern. This use of the holy name and authority of God was something of an important consideration for them. Some of the grimoires required a considerable period of prayers and even complete abasement before their deity in order to achieve the virtue of being able to act as his representative in this magical rite.

As Witches and Pagans, we don't have to worry about taking the name and authority of God in vain because we have assumed our personal godhead and through that sacred connection we will act with the authority and power to summon spirits to appear. It is a rather profound difference, but it requires us to carefully rewrite the invocation scripts so they reflect that we are acting as a deity and not by delegation, presumption, or appropriation. Curiously, if there is only a single deity as proposed in monotheism then one can only assume by delegation, presumption, or by appropriation. If there are many deities, as there are in polytheism, then each person also shares in that divinity as well. We thus summon spirits in the name of our personal deity through its power and authority wedded to our own willpower. That is a completely different paradigm, and it should be reflected in how we write our invocation scripts.

So, we don't refer to our deity in the third person; instead we refer to that being in the first person—we are that deity and we summon our target spirit through our own power, authority, and majesty. I know that this probably sounds a bit egotistical or startlingly different than what you have been expecting or previously read, but we must represent our spirituality as it currently exists instead of using a model based on Renaissance Christianity. Therefore, how we word our invocation script will be different than how a monotheist might write it.

Then there is the matter of using some kind of barbarous words of evocation to help set the mood. I have found it important to use some arcane and antique magical expressions to make the invocation script unique and unusual, and also to empower it. Using strange-sounding words has been a staple of the grimoire tradition going back to antiquity. Scholars call these words the *verba ignota* or the unknown language. Often these words are garbled forms of the names of gods, goddesses, demigods, or other famous entities (for example, the great serpent Agathodaimon). As these names were passed down through the centuries, most became unfamiliar to whoever used them; they became distorted and garbled until they were almost unrecognizable. Needless to say these lists of names became a kind of distorted language, only lacking in any type of syntax or intelligible language structure to make it a full language. It is up to you whether or not you want to use any of these words in your invocation script; if you do, you will have to practice how to pronounce them until they can be read or recited fluidly and effortlessly.

I thought that it would be helpful to show some examples of what invocation scripts look like from various old grimoires. Perhaps we can then put together our own version (based on Witchcraft and Paganism) using elements from each that will suffice as a model for you to use when it comes time for you to write your version of this script. This will also help you realize that there is a lot of published and Internet material out there about summoning spirits, perhaps more than in any other time in history.

Our first example comes from the oldest known collection of magical rituals known as the Greek Magical Papyri or PGM. These spells and rituals were written on a massive papyrus scroll in Koine Greek, Coptic, and Demotic Egyptian languages. They have been dated from around the first to the third centuries C.E. This particular invocation is a spell used to produce a divine revelation, and it is also used to invoke the "Serpent Faced God." The words of power are similar to those used in a number of the spells found in the book. When pronouncing these words of power, I would pronounce them phonetically, placing slight vowel sounds between difficult consonant clusters. The long vowel denotations in the words can be reproduced by lengthening and accenting the vowel sound.

[PGM XII lines 153–160][35]
"IAŌ IAŌ IAŌ I call upon you, Ptha Ra Ptha Iē Phtha
Oun Emēcha Erōchth Barōch Thorchtha Thōm Chaieouch
Archandabar Ōeaeō Ynēōch Ēra Ōn Ēlōph Bom Phtha
Athabrasia Abriasōth Barbarbelōcha Barbaiaōch; let there
be depth, breadth, length, brightness, Ablanathanalba
Abrasiaoua Akramma Chamarei Thōth Hōr Athōōpō.
Come in, lord, and reveal!"

Heptameron (Fourteenth century C.E.)

---

35 Hans Dieter Betz, *The Greek Magical Papyri in Translation—Including the Demotic Spells* (Chicago: University of Chicago Press, 1992), 159.

"Beralenensis, Baldachiensis, Paumachiae, and Apologiae Sedes, by the most mighty kings and powers, and the most powerful princes, genii, Liachidae, ministers of the Tartarean seat, chief prince of the seat of Apologiae, in the ninth legion, I invoke you, and by invoking, conjure you; and being armed with power from the supreme Majesty, I strongly command you, by Him who spoke and it was done, and to whom all creatures are obedient; and by this ineffable name, Tetragrammaton IHVH Jehovah, ... "[36]

Greater Key of Solomon (Sixteenth century C.E.)
"I conjure you, Oh Spirits, by the Power, the Wisdom and Virtue of the Spirit of God, by whose Divine Knowledge, by his Power, by His Greatness and His Unity, by the holy names of God. Which Adam, having named, he received the knowledge of all the Creatures. By the indescribable name Joel, which signals and conveys the unity of the Divine Nature, which Abel having pronounced, he was worthy to escape from the hands of Cain, his brother; by the Names of JEHOVA ELOHIM, which Noah, having pronounced, saved himself from the [Flood] Waters along with all his family."[37]

Grimorium Verum (Sixteenth century C.E.)
Oration: "Astrachios, Asach, Asarca, Abedumabal, Silat, Anabotas, Jesubilin, Scingin, Geneon, Domol, O Lord God, who art seated upon the heavens and regards the abyss, I pray that you deign to make me worthy of the power to conceive

---

36 Stephen Skinner, *The Fourth Book of Occult Philosophy by Henry Cornelius Agrippa*, edited with commentary (Berwick, ME: Ibis Press, 2005), 71.

37 Stephen Skinner and David Rankine, *The Veritable Key of Solomon (Sourceworks of Ceremonial Magic vol. 4)* (Woodbury, MN: Llewellyn Publications, 2008), 293.

my mind and then execute all that I wish to accomplish, through your aid, O God almighty, who lives and reigns for all the ages of the ages. Amen."

Invocation to Scirlin: "**Helon + Taul + Varf + Pan + Heon + Homonoreum + Clemialh + Serugeath + Agla + Tetragrammaton + Casoly +**"[38]

The Goetia of Dr. Rudd (Eighteenth century C.E.)
Invocation or Conjuration [of Sunday]: "**I conjure and confirm you. O you strong and holy Angels of God, in the name of Adonay, Eye, Eya who is he, who was who is, and shall be, Eye, Abraye, and in the name Saday, Cados, Cados, Cados, sitting high upon the Cherubim; and by the great name of the Same strong God and potent, and exalted upon all the heavens Eye, Saraye the Creator of Ages, who created the world, the heavens, the earth, the Sea, and all things that are therein in the first day, and sealed them with his holy name Phaa, …**"[39]

The Goetia of Aleister Crowley
(originally seventeenth century C.E.)
First Conjuration: "**I invoke and move thee, O thou, Spirit N.: and being exalted above ye in the power of the Most High, I say unto thee, Obey! In the name Beralenensis, Baldachiensis, Paumachia, and Apologiae Sedes: and of the mighty ones who govern, spirits, Liachidae and ministers of the House**

---

38 Joseph H. Peterson, *Grimorium Verum: A Handbook of Black Magic* (Scotts Valley, CA: CreateSpace Publishing, 2007), 33.

39 Skinner and Rankine, *The Goetia of Dr. Rudd,* 199.

of Death: and by the Chief Prince of Apologia in the Ninth Legion, I do invoke thee and by invoking conjure thee ... " [40]

[This invocation was obviously adapted from the invocation found in the earlier Heptameron, and Crowley translated it into the Enochian language to give it a greater gravitas.]

Grimoire Armadel (Eighteenth century C.E.)
Conjuration: "O Eternal Omnipotent God, Who hast formed every creature unto Thy praise and honour, and for the Ministry of Man: I beseech Thee to send unto me the Spirit [name] of [class or order] Order, who may inform and teach me concerning those things which I shall demand of him, nevertheless not my Will, but Thine, be done, through Thine Only-begotten Son Jesus Christ. Amen." [41]

As you can doubtlessly see, all of these invocation scripts are similar and many of them (but not all) have some kind of barbarous words of evocation. They are devout expressions of piety and while they formulate a type of profound submission to God, they also presume to employ the authority and power of the deity to conjure spirits to do whatever they want. This produces a moral quandary if the spirits are conjured by the sorcerer for illicit purposes, such as to sow enmity, murder, steal, seduce other peoples' partners, and to achieve dark and nefarious ends without any consequence.

What I am proposing is to formulate an invocation script that is bereft of Christian morality but maintains a true spiritual expression of

---

40   Aleister Crowley, *The Book of the Goetia of Solomon the King* (London: The Equinox Booksellers, 1976), 54.

41   Samuel L. MacGregor Mathers, *The Grimoire of Armadel* with Introduction by William Keith (New York: Weiser Books, 2001), 18.

polytheistic and magical ethics. This means that you are allowed to seek any end through the artifice of magic if you can justify it to yourself and your personal godhead. That alone will ensure that what you will do is ethical and just, because if it is otherwise, you will certainly reap the harshest consequences of your actions.

Here is how I would write up an invocation script using my personal godhead as the power and authority to command a spirit to appear. I would also liberate some of the words of power from the PGM invocation script since it represents a pantheistic kind of occult mindset that is truly relevant today.

> "I invoke and summon you, Oh Spirit *[Name or Name 'of' and Group Name]* to appear before me, in the name of my truest self as God, [*secret God Name*] and by the authority of their emissaries [*Names of Emissaries or Attributes*]. I call you from the Spirit World to this sacred place, properly prepared for you. I utter the sacred and powerful names so that you will come to me and know that I speak with the mouth of the Gods, and that my hands are the mighty hands of the Gods, and that my heart is like a great Serpent Lion breathing fire! Ptha Ra Ptha Iē Phtha Oun Emēcha Erōchth Barōch Thorchtha Thōm Chaieouch Archandabar Ōeaeō Ynēōch Ēra Ōn Ēlōph Bom Phtha Athabrasia Abriasōth Barbarbelōcha Barbaiaōch; let there be depth, breadth, length, brightness, Ablanathanalba Abrasiaoua Akramma Chamarei Thōth Hōr Athōōpō."

That is my version of the invocation script; you can take and modify it in whatever fashion you like to make it your own. The script works with any spirit name and its associated grouping or class, although you might want to write a specialized invocation script for a deity or demigod. You will also need to provide your secret God Name given to you by your personal Godhead or Higher Self, and you will need to discover a list of emissaries or attributes associated with your Godhead. For instance, the Egyptian god Horus has four sons that would be considered his emissaries. (These are Imsety, Duamutef, Hapi, and Qebehsenuef.) You can also think up four attributes of your Godhead that most represent his or her qualities as a deity. These attributes are not static and unchanging, since your personal Godhead will evolve and become more defined as you spiritually and magically evolve.

One last thing to cover are the steps associated with the Invocation phase, besides the obvious action of loudly reciting the invocation script. Here are the steps that you will undertake when performing the invocation.

1. Proceed to the shrine and unwrap the consecrated sigil.

2. Take the sigil to the center of the circle along with your wand and place it on the floor. Draw an invoking spiral over it (clockwise, outside to center). Get a small incense burner and place it next to the sigil and light an incense stick so that the sigil area has some smoking incense. Then take the wand and draw a deosil circle around the sigil and incense burner, starting in the east and ending in the east.

3. Kneel or sit before the sigil circle armed with the wand and recite or read the invocation script. As you read it, you begin to stand up and raise your arms up before you, drawing the spirit down into the circle to where the sigil is kept. You should read through it three times, with the last time being louder and more emphatic than the previous recitations.

4. Sit before the sigil circle to begin the next stage of the working.

Constraining the Spirit—Focusing and Manifesting the Apparition of the Spirit

Proceeding from the invocation to the constraining phase only occurs if the Witch is performing an evocation. If instead she has decided to perform an invocation because of the nature and status of the spirit then she would proceed with a communion step, which we will cover later in this chapter. For now let us assume that the Witch is performing an evocation and that she must now constrain the spirit into some form of apparition.

This is the most difficult part of the operation of summoning a spirit because it is where the Witch must focus her willpower at the point in the center of the circle and urge the spirit to manifest. She does this by repeating the spirit's name over and over in her mind and focuses her eyes on the sigil that has been placed in the center of the circle with its own incense burner. She would also be facing the shrine and drawing in the blessings and powers of her personal godhead who she has also fully assumed into herself. It is at this point that she enters into a trance state while continuing to call and urge the spirit to appear before her. At some point she closes her eyes and enters into a deeper trance state and once there she will likely fully realize the apparition of the target spirit. If she has developed her abilities to see and hear spirits, then she will begin to converse with the spirit and observe it manifesting into some form.

If, however, she neither sees nor hears anything, it doesn't automatically mean that the spirit has not manifested and that the summoning rite is a failure. What it may mean is that the Witch is unable to perceive the spirit for some reason. She can surface from her trance enough to take a single die or knucklebone that she keeps handy and throw it to the floor while formulating the question in her mind whether the spirit has appeared or not.

How you use dice or knucklebones to get answers to yes or no questions is very simple. For a single die you can use the number of dots to determine a range of possible yes or no answers. For instance, the numbers 1 and 2 would be a strong negative, 3 and 4 would be neutral (a non-answer), and 5 or 6 would be a strong positive. She should continue to throw the die to get either a strong positive or negative answer.

A "no" answer would indicate that the summoning rite, for whatever reason, had failed and should be abandoned. A "yes" answer would indicate that the spirit has manifested, but for some reason is unable to be perceived. At that point you can either renew your efforts to establish communication with the spirit or you can use the dice to help you determine what further actions are needed to remedy the situation. You could also consult with your higher self as your personal Godhead to help you resolve the issue. However, if you have spent months learning to see and hear spirits and to perceive the spirit world, then you will be able to sense the presence of the spirit and communicate with it in some internalized manner. One would assume that you had already been able to do this with your personal Godhead.

While it is possible that your first attempt to summon a spirit might fail due to something lacking in your preparations, if you have faithfully followed my recommendations for all of the preparation steps (and followed them for at least several months), then you will probably be successful. You should also consider that the formal invocation operation is typically preceded by a number of informal invocations and contacts, so success at performing informal operations would ensure the success for a formal operation. Anyway, we will continue our discussion under the assumption that you have successfully established communication with the target spirit.

Once you have successfully made contact with the target spirit and sense its presence and perhaps even see an apparition, you should proceed to have a dialogue with it in your mind and make absolutely certain that it is what it claims to be. Of course, the likelihood that this is some other spirit masquerading as your target spirit is quite unlikely since it is by the name and sigil that you have summoned it. Still, this formal but polite interrogation is useful in determining that the target spirit is fully active and capable of performing the task that you want it to accomplish.

Another potential task that is a part of this phase of the summoning is to make certain that the spirit will fully cooperate with you. If a spirit's nature or character is passionate, volatile, and even potentially hostile, then you will have to take a more aggressive approach to control it and make certain that it is willing to do your will. This is often a battle of wills, but you have an unbeatable combination because you had assumed your personal Godhead before the summoning was performed. All you have to do is to bring out that Godhead (by deliberately invoking its name in your internalized conversation with the spirit) and cause it to be focused on the spirit before you, and all potential problems will be immediately neutralized. I have had recourse to this trick in the past and it still amazes me how a difficult situation is quickly resolved by bringing my personal Godhead into the conflict—whatever was going on just ends then and there. After all, that is why we assume the Godhead before performing a summoning—it is there to ensure that we are guided and protected at all times.

In some instances, if the conjured spirit is a lesser earth-based entity, then the Witch can constrain it into a bottle or some other kind of container. The bottle or container should be decorated with the sigil of the spirit and other designs, and a bit of earth or a relic (pebble, leaf, or some other artifact from the spirit's locality) can be put into the bottle to establish it as a physical link. Then, instead of conjuring the spirit into the center of the circle, the Witch will focus and make the spirit manifest into the bottle, sealing it with wax or a stopper once that is accomplished. Then the spirit can be bound with various agreements or pacts to perform certain tasks while in the bottle by projecting through it. Unsealing the bottle releases the spirit, but if it is properly constrained and bound it will return to the bottle when ordered to do so. I would advise you to select only lower level local earth spirits to perform this kind of work. Choosing a more powerful entity and then dominating it in this manner might provoke some very serious blowback if the spirit ever found a way to escape (and it will).

Once the manifestation of the spirit has been completely verified, then the Witch proceeds to the next phase of the working. However, if for some reason the summoning has failed, then the Witch proceeds directly to the last phase, which is where she releases the spirit. One cannot assume that even a failed invocation has not produced some results that will need to released and dismissed before the working can be properly ended.

Binding—Agreement or Pact with the Spirit

At this point in the summoning rite, the Witch has already established (through informal contact) that the target spirit is capable and also willing to perform a task that the Witch desires. She will also likely have an idea of what the spirit wants in return for performing her task. This agreement, called the quid-pro-quo between Witch and spirit represents the whole justification and basis for the formal evocation of the spirit. What is required here is a formal agreement for the spirit to do a task for the Witch during an established time period, and if that task is completed then she will honor the spirit's request for something in return. Typically, this obligation on the part of the Witch will be an offering of some kind made to the sigil of the spirit placed on the shrine.

The agreement must be mutual and it must also be kept if the spirit fulfills its part. If during the period of time agreed upon the desired thing doesn't occur then the agreement is null and void; but the Witch should make certain that absolutely nothing happened even remotely like the desired objective. What I typically do is to make an initial minor offering (as a sweetener) to be followed by the main offering once the objective is verified as having been accomplished. I would also recommend keeping your objective simple and singularly clear. Ask for exactly that one thing and nothing else. Make certain that what you are asking can actually occur in the timeframe that you are asking it to be accomplished. Then when it does occur, make certain that you make the offering at the first opportunity— don't wait or procrastinate.

We will look at the pact or agreement in greater detail in the next chapter when we cover information about spirits, how they function, and what one can reasonably expect from developing a relationship with them.

Once the spirit and the Witch agree to the term of the pact or arrangement, then the matter is completed and the spirit should be released. However, if the objective was to gain some information, direction, or divination then it will likely happen very quickly. This kind of objective can be met either instantaneously or within the next 24 to 48 hours. Still, the offering should be given once the objective has been met regardless of how soon it happens. So it is possible that the offering may have to be made during the very working used to summon the spirit. Therefore, an allotment of time should be made (as well as the required items used) to give this offering at the end of the working just before the release.

Communion for an Invocation

If you performed an invocation instead of an evocation rite, then once the summoned spirit becomes present, you are obliged to celebrate that event with a meal that is blessed and shared. Having already performed some informal invocations to engage and access this entity, you will know what special requirements this deity will expect from you in order to be properly and respectfully vetted into the pantheon of collective deities associated with your shrine. Of course, this is only true if you are adding this entity to your shrine, since there are circumstances when that would not be desired or required.

While your own personal Godhead will be the dominant entity in this collective, you will likely add additional deities and spirits to this special group represented in some manner within your shrine. Not only will you be expected to serve the periodic needs of your personal deity, but you will also have to serve the needs of these additional entities because they will all be part of your polytheistic religious discipline.

One important thing you will need to consider when deciding to invoke a deity or godlike entity is whether or not to add them to your shrine. You should never perform an invocation of a deity, demigod, ancestor, or holy intermediary without at least considering whether or not you intend to add it to your religious collective and give it periodic offerings.

While this is not absolutely required, if you have any intention of accessing this entity periodically or even regularly then you should add it to the deities that are part of your shrine collective.

If you develop a relationship over time with a deity or godlike entity then it will be as if you had an activated numinous presence of that being functioning as part of your shrine. While it is acceptable to invoke a deity from whom you want something, and giving it a communion offering can establish an informal quid-pro-quo, it is better to summon a spirit for such a task than seeking the one-time help of a deity. Some deities will not approve of being used in this manner while others will not have a problem with it.

Also, keep in mind that deities are more high level and are less inclined to or capable of engaging in mundane or material aspirations. Of course, you don't have to follow this rule when invoking benign emissaries or intermediaries, such as archangels—they will accept a quid-pro-quo communion offering.

Therefore, prior to performing such an invocation rite, you will need to keep ready a special meal consisting of food and drink prepared for this occasion. You will need to research and know what kind of food and drink the deity will find acceptable as an offering, and then prepare it before the working.

Figure 19: drawing showing a shrine and offering table set before it

As in the constraining phase of evocation, you will have to determine if the invocation was successful and to what extent the deity has manifested. You will also need to make the judgment that this entity has indeed appeared before you in the expected manner. I have never performed an invocation rite that didn't quickly produce the results that I was seeking since such entities are very disposed toward appearing when called. This is particularly true if you have an offering to make that is acceptable and pleasing to it. The idea is to share an offering with the deity that will produce a bond of love and faith between you and it, therefore beginning a process of building up a strong and useful relationship. Giving regular offerings will ensure that you have the right and privilege to ask for favors in return, where a successful outcome to your request will produce a greater bounty of further offerings.

This is what you will do to celebrate a communion rite with a fully invoked and manifested deity. You will take the sigil and the incense burner and place them on the shrine with reverence and loving care, bowing low before it. You will have previously set up a small table before the shrine and have placed on it the food, drink, flowers in a vase, incense holder, and candles. Light the candles and some incense and bow before the laden table so that you are completely prostrate for a few moments. Then get up, look upon the food, and say a prayer to the deity (looking and gesturing to the sigil) inviting it to bless these offerings specially made for it. Then take the sigil in your right hand, place it over the burning incense to catch the perfumed smoke, and imagine a ray of light descending from the sigil to touch the food, flowers, and drink. Then replace the sigil on the shrine and bow once again before the food, saying a prayer of thanksgiving to the deity for blessing the offering.

Once this is done, you can sit and meditate for a short time before the table, and then you can partake of the food and drink, making certain to leave a portion of it behind for the deity. Then you should meditate for a while on what you have received from the deity in terms of blessings, and realize that a divine connection is now established between it and you. A communion rite produces a powerful bond between you and the invoked deity, momentarily making you and that entity one.

Proceed to the release phase, being mindful that you are not really letting the connection lapse since you now have a religious responsibility to make offerings to this newly installed deity, if that is your intention. You will only have to perform the steps that seals the gateway and the vortex. Later on you can find a suitable statue or physical symbol of the deity that will be a part of your religious collective represented in your personal shrine, provided, of course, that you are making this entity a part of your personal pantheon.

Release—Permission or License to Depart

Giving a spirit its release, or "license to depart" as it is usually called, is where the summoned spirit is allowed to leave the presence of the Witch who summoned it and go about its business. A release is stated as the formal declaration of departure. It is spoken out loud to the spirit, but done in a thankful and respectful manner, giving the spirit a heartfelt farewell. However, this license to depart is also given under certain conditions; that it has been expressed by the conjuror and understood by the spirit as the beginning of a periodic visitation and a working relationship.

A Witch may have need of the evoked spirit again in the future, once the current task is done, so she seeks to build a kind of connection or link so that summoning it again will be easier and simpler. What can help this connection work is where the spirit is asked to give a mark or sign (in addition to the sigil of its name) that can be drawn on a piece of consecrated parchment and used to gain immediate access to the spirit. Not all spirits might be so inclined to allow for this kind of connection, but for those who do, it can be an invaluable part of a Witch's regalia to have spirit servitors that she can call into manifestation whenever needed.

Therefore, there are two things that are done in this final phase of the summoning rite, and that is making a pact to allow for easy access to the spirit whenever needed and also the releasing of the spirit from its constraint, if it was evoked.

Here are the steps that you should follow to perform this spell of releasing.

1. Ask the spirit if it is willing to give its mark or character so that it might be called whenever needed. If it is willing then receive the mark—you can write it down when it is shown to you or carefully memorize it. (Optional for an invocation rite.)

2. Bow before the spirit's sigil and thank it for attending and agreeing to take upon itself your special task.

3. Give assurance that you will fully abide by the agreement that has been forged, by your honor as a Witch and devotee of your personal Godhead. (Optional for an invocation rite.)

4. Recite the release script three times.

5. Draw a sealing spiral (outside widdershins to inside) over the sigil and the incense burner. Put out the incense, and replace the sigil on the shrine if it was evoked.

Then perform the following steps to complete the working.

1. Closing the western gateway

2. Sealing the Rose Ankh vortex

3. Grounding

The release script typically looks like this text, although you can write your own version. If you performed an invocation rite then you would leave out the word "Spirit" and omit the second sentence.

> "Oh Spirit [Name], I thank you for your blessed attendance and I am grateful that you have honored my God [Name of Personal Godhead] with your presence and cooperation. May I bless you through my God and therefore give you license to depart from my presence in peace and goodwill. I wish you fond farewell and many blessings."

We have now discussed all of the phases that you need to follow in order to successfully complete either an invocation or an evocation rite. However, we need to discuss in greater detail the nature of spirits, their classes and collective groupings, how to properly determine and then commit them to a desired objective (quid-pro-quo or pact), and also discuss the nature and symbolic features of the Spirit World. There is much yet to know about spirits and their domain, so let us move on to the next important topic.

7

Spirit Lists, Managing Different Spirits, and Traveling the Spirit World

Be hole, be dust, be dream, be wind/Be night, be dark,
be wish, be mind/Now slip, now slide, now move
unseen/Above, beneath, betwixt, between.

NEIL GAIMAN, *THE GRAVEYARD BOOK*

We have covered the mechanisms and techniques used for performing an invocation or an evocation, and now we need to delve deeper into the nature of the spirits we would target for such an operation. We have gone over the basic hierarchical structure of the spirits and where they reside in the three-tiered spirit world. Still, there is much more to examine and reveal about spirits in order for a potential Witch conjuror to be able to pick the right spirit for a specific task. In all of this work, it is critically important to perform a series of informal summoning rites. This is done to fully develop a complete familiarity with the target spirit before the formal summoning. Such an engagement will help the Witch make certain that the target spirit can indeed assist her to achieve a given objective and that it is willing to do so for a specific compensation.

It is also important to know that if you decide to perform an invocation instead of an evocation because of the status of the spirit in question, then doing such an act may pose certain obligations that should be either taken up or demurred. Not every invocation has to result in you taking upon yourself another entity to add to your collection installed in the shrine, thereby requiring periodic offerings. You do have a choice as to whether to include the spirit in your shrine collective or not. For instance, you don't have to install archangels or other exalted angelic beings in your shrine unless these entities are going to be a part of your spiritual and religious alignment. The same is true of other types of entities, such as chthonic deities, demon princes, or infernal chiefs. However, if you do include any of these entities in your shrine for a specific practical purpose, then you will also shift your spiritual alignment as well. You could, as a result, become an "angelolater" or a "demonolater" if you have a bias in one direction or the other. There is nothing wrong with either perspective. In fact a Witch, who has no vested alignment with Abrahamic theology, could build an alignment with both selected demons and angels. We will discuss this in greater detail later in this chapter.

One of the most important things that anyone, Witch or Pagan, who seeks to conjure spirits must understand is that the usual cultural tropes of "angels are good and demons are bad" should be completely abandoned. While I realize that this is probably very difficult and it would seem that we are hard-wired to accept this fallacy, it is a product of monotheistic duality that bears no resemblance to the actual spirit world as experienced by a Witch or Pagan. Things are really much more complex and nuanced than what anyone who is subscribing to the Abrahamic myths would be willing to admit. So, the Western cultural heritage of the entire domain of angels is available to the Witch conjuror for her to use, and so is the same cultural heritage for the domain of demons. I am not advocating either one because that will be something that you will determine through your own research and magical workings. What I will emphasize is that we, as Witches and Pagans, must examine these issues with an open mind and put away our prejudices in order to engage the Spirit World as someone completely free of the religious and cultural biases of the Abrahamic faiths.

What this means is that a Witch conjuror can engage with any spirit she chooses without carrying preconceived notions or prohibitions. Certainly this kind of fuzzy thinking had no bearing on the great witches and conjurors of antiquity, so we should also abandon it as limiting and burdensome. We are therefore released from this baggage to do our conjuring work in whatever manner suits us, acknowledging that we must take responsibility for our actions and whatever occurs.

Your personal Godhead, familiar spirit, and higher self is the first and foremost deity installed in your shrine. This is always the starting point for the erstwhile Witch conjuror, but it seldom remains that way for very long. Over time you will accumulate other entities represented by statues or other symbolic markers that you will have to make offerings to on a periodic basis. Other spirits and deities that could be added to the shrine would be household spirits, such as the lares and penates of your hearth and home. However, I would recommend that you carefully consider and completely justify each case individually before you add new entities to this enshrined collection.

What is installed in your shrine is a representation of your particular spiritual alignment, and expanding this alignment for any reason should be carefully considered before actually doing it. One of the things you will need to consider is the implication or effect that the combination of entities will have on your overall spiritual alignment. More importantly you will need to understand how these entities will work together as a unified group aiding you in your spiritual and magical progress. This is where your personal Godhead can help you make decisions since it is the premier deity in your shrine and it will be able to help you determine if adding some entity is either a good idea or a bad one.

Since you will be making offerings to all of the symbolic representations of these entities on a regular basis, each and every one of them should be expected to give you something in return. You also have the option of retiring an entity and its symbolic marker from the shrine if it no longer serves any kind of purpose in your work; but you should do this task with the highest respect and reverence. You should make certain that the entity knows why you are doing this and what it means. I would recommend in such a situation that you give the entity a feast and offer it a heartfelt farewell when performing this action. It is possible that you might need this entity again in your work, and it is also foolish to make spiritual enemies either by carelessness or negligence.

You have options, then, whether or not to add an entity that you have invoked to your shrine. You can either admit an entity to your spiritual house (as the shrine represents) or remain neutral. If you perform an invocation where you choose not to add that entity to your shrine, then you should at least give it a proper offering and direct it to perform some objective for you. This agreement is not backed up with constraining and binding operations as part of an evocation, so the agreement is more of a friendly and casual one. It is always possible that you might get more in return than you gave in an offering. In that case you might consider making another offering. However, taking a friendly but non-aligned stance with a specific invoked entity is something you can do without any adverse consequences just so long as it receives the initial offering for the request that you have made to it.

As for the classes of spirits that would be summoned using an invocation rite instead of an evocation, these are any deities, demigods, heroes, great ancestors (cultural ancestors), spiritual or genetic ancestors, and local fairy or earth spirit royalty (heads of earth-spirit collectives). Included with this list are archangels, super archangels (such as seraphim and cherubim), demon princes, or infernal chiefs. All of these entities should be invoked instead of evoked because to constrain and bind them would be considered offensive and denigrating. You can choose any of these entities to be invoked or installed in your shrine or you can be neutral and just establish a temporary relationship.

As for ancestors, it is a good idea to acknowledge and to pay certain homage to your genetic ancestors. I would recommend setting up a shelf or the top of a bookcase or fireplace mantle with pictures of your lineal ancestors. However, I would recommend only including pictures of your linear ancestors in your shrine who would agree and assist you in your magical work. In my case, none of my ancestors would approve of my magical work so I have omitted any of them from my shrine. I do have a special place for all of my ancestors, but it is located away from my magical temple and shrine.

In additional to your genetic ancestors, there are also spiritual ancestors associated with your Pagan or Witchcraft tradition. Pictures of these individuals are exactly what you need to represent your spiritual traditions and their associated alignments. Installing a picture of Gerald B. Gardner, Alexander Sanders, Victor and Cora Anderson, or anyone else representing your religious and magical tradition would be very appropriate. It also means that once you install such a founder in your shrine, you should behave in a respectful and reverential manner toward them. Whatever flaws and defects they had when they were alive are to be overlooked. Instead, you should focus on their legacy and what they represent to your tradition.

You can also consider adding legendary individuals such as Apollonius of Tyanna, Hercules, Perseus, Cú Chulainn, or anyone that you particularly admire to your shrine, keeping in mind that you should develop a personal rapport with these heroes and that they should add something to your overall spiritual alignment. Demigods such as Hermes Trismegistus, Asclepius, Adonis, or Agathodaimon could also be added, but once again you will have to establish a rapport with any entity added to your shrine. I would recommend that you consider performing an invocation for any deity, demigod, hero, or great ancestor you add to the shrine. Where I would draw the line is with genetic ancestors, since you have a "blood" connection with those entities.

All of the entities installed in your shrine deserve and require periodic offerings of some kind. What I would recommend is that you have a feast once a month and give some of that feast as an offering to all of the spirits—food, drink, and whatever else. I would also include daily incense offerings, flowers, lit candles, and some kind of religious observation. This can be increased to include some kind of religious liturgy performed once a week and also on occasions prior to a working or when you need the intercession of one or any of these entities during a life crisis. As the priest and congregation of your own personal polytheistic cult, you are obligated and expected to periodically and (hopefully) regularly give offerings to the entities installed in your shrine. Remember, the more you put into your shrine then the more active those entities will be in assisting you and also giving you blessings and good fortune.

Spirit Lists—Classes and Groups of Spirits

This brings us to the discussion of the different lists, classes, and groups of spirits available for the Witch conjuror to use in her work. Most of these lists are derived from the old grimoires and documents of the previous ages and have evolved over time. Some of these lists involving the same classes or groups of spirits will differ and even contradict each other. What I would like to do is to provide you with a more simplified rendition of these lists and their sources, allowing you to absorb this information with the caveat that you will have to perform some rather extensive research to fully vet some of these lists.

It is for this reason that the lists I have provided are just that, lists of names without any specific characteristics or functions. I omitted this information because what is in the old grimoires and associated written material is so antiquated and biased that it is practically useless.

For instance, some of the Goetic demons are reputed to assist one in delivering instant messages from one individual to another, supplying rapid transportation (flying) or any other seemingly miraculous feat, such as they might have been conceived in the previous age. These supposed miracles are now readily provided today thanks to advanced technology, thereby nullifying the miracle the demon could provide. The lists that contain the lurid descriptions of the demons and their supposed abilities are very much out of date and not at all helpful.

What I think is more important is to engage a target spirit in a given class through an informal summoning and then seek to find out everything that you can about that class and also the particular spirit itself. This may require you to perform this operation against a number of spirits before you decide on one to evoke. It may seem like a time-consuming process to determine the nature and character of spirits, and it is; but it will produce valid and relevant information instead of information that is antique and heavily biased. You can still research these spirits and collect the information that exists about them in the old grimoires, but you will have to take that information with a grain of salt, knowing that it is likely misleading or even completely wrong. The spirits themselves are always the final and best source of valid information about them.

One of the most important resources that you will need to acquire and use on a regular basis is the book *A Dictionary of Angels: Including the Fallen Angels* by Gustav Davidson. Many of the spirit lists I have developed are to be found in the appendix of that work, and I highly recommend reading that part of the book thoroughly because it contains so much useful information. One of things that you will find when reading this section of the book is that the various authorities, whether

Christian or Jewish, didn't agree on any definitive list of angels belonging to any class or group. There are variances between these lists; some are quite different. All you need to understand is that not one of them is the one and only "true" list.

You are going to have to make some judgments on your own. This means that you will have to build up your own list based on whatever version or combination of versions appeal to you or seems most useful. This is exactly what I did to come up with the spirit lists that I use for my own work. Still, you have a slight advantage because you will have my lists as a starting point, if and when you attempt to navigate this very complex subject. Otherwise, you are welcome to use the lists straight from the antique sources, and you can use *Dictionary of Angels* to help you research any entity that you wish to invoke or evoke.

Another useful book is the *Dictionary of Demons: Names of the Damned* by Michelle Belanger, which contains a dictionary of all of the diabolic and demonic spirits. Of course, this book would only be useful if you were interested or at least curious about various fallen spirits. The correspondences in the back of the book are particularly useful. Since I have maintained that the so-called class of fallen or diabolic spirits cannot be judged using Christian, Jewish, or Islamic religious values (particularly because we are Witches or Pagans) then this book is probably at least worth an examination.

Other valuable sources of information about spirits are to be found in the books *The Complete Magician's Tables* by Stephen Skinner and *The Qabalah of Aleister Crowley* consisting of the writings of Aleister Crowley. The most important book in that collection is *Liber 777*, which contains the various Qabalistic tables of correspondences. While Crowley's version of the tables of correspondence is more difficult to understand and use even though it is considered the definitive work, the book by Stephen Skinner is much more accessible and easier to use. In these books you will find all of the tables of various spirits and associated attributes, some of which are organized into the sephiroth and pathways of the Tree of Life. These four books represent the bulk of the material that I have used to derive my own lists of spirits, so where possible they should be purchased and used by you for your work.

I have also previously recommended that you should begin your work as a Witch conjuror by engaging and contacting the various spirits, deities, and entities that reside in your locality. You may decide that this project is all that you need to do, and that invoking or evoking angels or demons isn't something that you want to pursue. I fully understand that perspective and I can find no fault with it. There are plenty of spirits in your local area that occupy the three domains of the spirit world, and they can be used to perform most of the tasks you might need to accomplish.

However, as I have pointed out, it is also good to take on challenges and to fully explore the spirit world, both the local area as well as the more iconic and traditional areas. Also, I believe that demons and angels can perform certain tasks and represent a degree of spiritual power, knowledge, and wisdom that would be far greater than the spirits and deities you would find in your local area. Angels and demons are more universal, so they would also have a greater reach and effectiveness than local entities. This is just my opinion, of course, based on my years of experience, but the ultimate decision is yours.

If you decide that you don't want to traffic with angels and demons, you can skip this section and move on to the next. What I will be imparting here won't be relevant to you or your work, but if you are interested then I invite you to continue to read. What I can't do is supply you a list of spirits, deities and other entities that reside in your local area. You will have to develop that list of spirits and its associated attributes, functions, and characteristics by yourself.

I also won't include a list of the spirits or angels associated with the elementals and planetary spirits, angels, and demigods. These spirits are an integral part of the elemental and planetary systems of magic; such methods and techniques are beyond the scope of this work and therefore are not included in these lists. This omission also includes the various spirits of the Enochian system of magic. I believe that any student who wants to include these spirits in their workings can learn the requisite magical systems that would underlie their employment.

The full list of all the spirits can be found in Appendix One at the back of this work.

Evocation Considerations

An evocation is performed for spirits that are not deities, demigods, ancestors, celestial intermediaries, or household deities/spirits. That means in the spirit lists presented in the appendix the candidates for evocation are the decan angels, the Ha-Shem angels, Goetic demons, angels and demons of the Theurgia-Goetia, angelic rulers of the lunar mansions, and the chiefs of the Nephilim. Any earth-based spirits, underworld spirits, or aerial spirits that are not of the higher class of deities, demigods, or celestial intermediaries would certainly be the kind of entities you would perform an evocation for summoning.

All of these angels, demons, and spirits have a specific function as a class and an additional capability as an individual in that class. Some of these spirits are qualified by the very number of total entries in the table of their class, while others represent just a collective grouping. As a rule of thumb, angels are evoked for the purpose of gaining specific knowledge, insights, or even a prophetic vision about some topic, issue, or possibility desired by the conjuror. Earth spirits and demons are evoked to achieve a specific material goal or end. They can also provide knowledge but typically are much more proficient at making things happen in certain circumstances.

Demons are particularly adept at cutting through all of the niceties and social protocols to achieve a certain goal, regardless of the harshness or even disastrous consequences for that object to be realized.[42] It is for this reason that an evocation of a demon is something that should be clearly worked out and examined through divination at a deep level. It is also important to develop the language of the agreement or pact in a manner that ensures simplicity, clarity, and objectivity. You will want to avoid ambiguity, ambivalence, vagueness, or logical errors that can introduce loopholes. I have heard a common story in occult social circles that tells what can befall someone who has made a pact with a demon that was ambiguous or unclear. It is also a classic morality tale told many times about the apparent pitfalls when making deals with the Devil. You will want to avoid any possible interpretation of your agreement other than that which you have unequivocally requested—nothing more or less. This is a precaution, and it is one that you should use when making a pact or agreement with any spirit regardless of class.

This is why it is important to keep your objective simple and clear, whatever it is. Ask for just one thing. If you are successful then you can ask for something else the next time you engage that spirit, since this interaction will foster a positive relationship between both of you. What can help you determine how to state your objective is to perform informal summoning rites and seek out not only what the spirit is willing to do for you, but also what you need to offer to the spirit in return. It's similar to finding how much something costs before you attempt to buy it.

Before you perform an evocation, you need to know not only what you want from the spirit but what you are willing to offer in return. This is the basis of the agreement or pact between you and the spirit, and it is something that should be negotiated. You might find yourself haggling

---

42 Of course, demons represent a considerable variance of behavior, from benign to overtly hostile. So the end result of an evocation of a demon will also vary considerably from one to the other, depending on the character of the entity summoned.

with the spirit during these informal connections since it might ask for something that you are unwilling to pay, or conversely, you might be asking the spirit to do something that it cannot do. Ultimately, you will find out what the spirit is willing to do and what you are willing to offer in return. The final version of this agreement should be written down on parchment and even consecrated.

In addition to the quid-pro-quo agreement, you will also need to set a deadline for when this objective should be completed. If your request is not fulfilled in the time that you specified, then the agreement is voided. You are not obligated to fulfill your part of the bargain if the spirit has not fulfilled its part. However, you need to carefully evaluate everything that has happened during the interval of time up to the deadline in order to determine if the request has indeed not been completed. Sometimes a request can be fulfilled in a very subtle and indirect manner, particularly if the request is something that is not tangible or obvious. It is important for you to reward the spirit if it helps you accomplish your goal.

Most requests are typically quite dramatic if they happen to be fulfilled through the magic of spirits. This is because the conjuror is seeking to make something physically tangible occur in the material world. In such instances it is pretty clear if the objective is successfully achieved, but other areas might be more intangible and require greater scrutiny. What I am referring to as subtle or intangible results are those that are focused internally on one's personality, intrinsic self, or a deeper connection with the spiritual world. Seeking love, money, employment opportunities, restitution, physical healing, or some other material thing or condition is simple to judge; but seeking wisdom, spiritual redemption, insights into a perplexing problem, clarity, psychological healing, or even justice for some wrong endured can be more subjective and difficult to determine.

You should also be aware of the simple fact that like all magical workings, you will need to perform the various mundane steps and actions that will ensure you achieve your objective. Never ask a spirit to do something that you are unwilling to even try to achieve by yourself. All endeavors assisted and blessed by magical workings that involve summoning a spirit are a partnership between you and the spirit. Because of this partnership, there is no excuse for you not doing everything in your power to achieve a goal even when aided by a spirit. Therefore, when examining a working that has failed to deliver the expected results you will discover whether the failure was due to you, the spirit, or both.

Technically speaking, you don't have to reward a spirit if an objective fails to materialize in the allotted time, but it is quite another matter if you refuse to give your offering to a spirit if the cause of the failure was completely yours. This represents the added complexity when working spirit magic that doesn't factor in when you are working magic using your own resources. In many cases you will likely find yourself rewarding a spirit if it indeed helped you, even though the expected outcome didn't materialize. Being able to determine this subtlety is the beginning of wisdom in this kind of working. (I would recommend a certain generosity when dealing with spirits; be quick to reward and honor a spirit for its help. Doing so will help you develop your relationship with other spirits and the spirit world as a whole.)

Basically, an agreement or pact with a spirit consists of five parts. These five parts need to be worked out in detail before you perform a formal evocation.

1. Objective, outcome, or request
2. Spirit's obligation (what you want the spirit to do)
3. Your obligation (what mundane steps are you going to take)
4. Spirit offering if the outcome is successful

5. Deadline for the objective to be realized

As I have said previously, formalize this pact by writing the completed form, in five parts, on a piece of parchment and then consecrate it, just like you did for the sigil. This makes the objective of the working a magical and sacralized object as well.

Choosing a Date for the Working

When all of the components for this working are being realized, one of the last things to do is to schedule the working. The summoning will be performed in a single evening, but the preparation may start days before. It depends on how much you have to prepare (first workings take the most time, of course) and how intense you want the working to be when the appointed time arrives.

While some magicians go through elaborate processes of consulting astrological transits versus their natal chart, and even consulting a progressed natal chart and then analyzing the positions and angular relationships between the planets on the day or hour of the working, I believe that you can choose a date using far less data. Some also choose to use the planetary hours to determine an auspicious time for the working, but I believe that you can be more flexible because of the nature of the magic you are working.

The phases of the moon have a greater influence on spirit magic performed in the spirit world than any other planet, in my opinion. This means that you can follow the four phases of the moon, or better yet, the eight stages of the lunation cycle. Knowledge of the lunation cycle is quite common, from astrologers to farmers. However, I will show it here in tabular form so you can examine it for yourself.

Lunation Cycle Table [43]

Lunation Type	Interval Degrees	Key Word	Description
New Moon Type	0–45	Emergence	Subjective, impulsive, novelty
Crescent Type	45–90	Expansion	Self-assertion, self-confidence
First Quarter Type	90–135	Action	Crisis in action, strong-willed
Gibbous Moon Type	135–180	Overcoming	Clarification, revelation & illumination
Full Moon Type	180–225	Fulfillment	Objectivity, formulation, manifestation
Disseminating Type	225–270	Demonstration	Disseminator of ideas, populist, teacher
Last Quarter Type	270–315	Re-orientation	Crisis in consciousness, inflexibility
Balsamic Type	315–360	Release	Transition, seed-state, germination

As you can see from the table above, the best times for performing a formal invocation or evocation is when the moon is waxing or increasing from the new moon. The lunation types for this period are crescent, first quarter, and gibbous, represented by the key words *expansion, action,* and *overcoming.* The date of the working should be at some point

---

43 See Dane Rudhyar's *The Lunation Cycle: A Key to the Understanding of Personality* (New York: Aurora Press, 1986), 50–56. I have used the text to distill the entries in this table.

during the gibbous moon (overcoming) type just before the full moon (fulfillment). Divination is best performed around the last quarter to the balsamic types, where the keywords *reorientation* and *release* describe the energies appropriately. The Disseminating lunation type is best for establishing deadlines, where the energies of fulfillment (full moon) become demonstrated in physical fact. I would set the deadline based on lunar cycles, with the least being one lunar cycle from the working during the "dissemination" type. (The exception, of course, would be the invocation or evocation of entities that are wholly chthonic or reside in full darkness. These should be summoned at or just before the new moon during the balsamic or new moon lunation types.)

As for what days to schedule the working and the preparation, I leave that detail to whatever schedule you can support. This will be shaped by your mundane life and its requirements, which are just as important as the magical workings that you will do. I typically performed my workings on the weekend because I didn't have to work and it was a period where I could devote time to my magic without adversely affecting anything else in my life. You will have to work out when, where, and how you will do your magical workings; but if there is enough desire to do this work then the time to do it will always be found.

Considerations about Angelolatry and Demonolatry

As a Witch you have the advantage of choosing your allies and determining your spiritual and religious alignment. Your liturgical responsibilities are not forced on you by law or convention; they are voluntarily assumed. This means that you are free, but if you work with the spirit theory of magic you will find it necessary to establish alignments and acquire spiritual alliances that will require specific liturgical obligations. You will be obligated to give offerings to your spiritual allies on a periodic and regular schedule. These allies, including your personal Godhead, will be represented in some fashion in your shrine. Over time, you will find that your obligations will grow, but it will also sort itself out to a set of deities, demigods, and celestial intermediaries. Your collective may be diverse (which is typical) or it might be more exclusive. An exclusive pantheon can be represented by a specific tradition or culture, or it can be determined by an excess of angels or demons, making you an angelolater or a demonolater.

I consider angels and demons to be various forms of intermediaries, where angels might be considered aerial spirits and demons might be considered chthonic spirits. Either definition is probably too simplistic, since both groups function as intermediaries and so there really isn't that much difference between them. In my workings I have found that some angels are forceful, overpowering, and even a bit dangerous (such as the seraphim and cherubim), while some demons I have evoked are friendly and helpful. However, the key to your alignment is the class and association of the spirits that reside in your shrine. If you have installed the super archangels and archangels in your shrine, you might be limited to what other entities would work with that collective. The same thing would be true if you had installed the seven demon princes and four demon chiefs, along with Scirlan, such would be the case if you were working with the True Grimoire. When you choose to heavily align yourself to one faction or the other then you are practicing either angelolatry or demonolatry.

To choose one of these alignments is understandable, but it will have an impact on your magic and the kind of spirits you will summon. It also means that the deities of light or darkness will also be part of your spiritual alignment. The kind of magic you will wield as perceived by the public will also be biased in the same manner. This will happen regardless of what you do in life or how you act toward others because you will be regularly making obligatory offerings to the entities installed in your shrine. There is nothing *wrong* with this approach because it happens to represent a left-hand path (or right-hand path) approach to the practice of spirit-based magic. However, there is a third way; it is the direction that I have chosen.

My alignments are to my Pagan deities, some of whom are very private and meaningful only to me. I also admit certain alignments associated with my tradition of Witchcraft and the kind of magic I perform. When dealing with angels and demons, however, I don't take any specific side. I have invoked and evoked many from both sides, and what I've learned is that you don't need to be aligned to these entities in order to engage with them. You do need to be true to your own spiritual practices and traditional theology, which is another way of saying that you need to be religious in your own way. The angels don't belong to the adherents of the Abrahamic faith, and the demons don't belong to their adversaries. All of these entities are part of our cultural and spiritual heritage; but they tend to respond to us based on our beliefs and attitudes toward them. Our spiritual beliefs and religious practices shape our experiences with all spirits. If I consider myself to be a Witch who is not aligned to either light or darkness, I am free from the polarizing effects of monotheistic duality, and I consider that the optimal way for me to function. In fact it gives me the opportunity to wield the powers of both light and darkness, which is how I envision Witchcraft.

When considering your spiritual alignments, be aware that your choices do have an effect and also consequences. Don't choose a faction unless such a choice is powerfully meaningful and significant to you. Based on what I have said previously, this sort of choice is difficult; it takes time to gracefully change and evolve your spiritual alignment based on the entities installed in your shrine. You can't discard spiritual allies like you can superficial social acquaintances, like on Facebook. You have to justify your actions and you have to make these changes in a gentle and graceful manner unless you want to cause a great deal of disharmony or even some major disasters in your life. Never make a spirit angry unless it is altogether unavoidable, and if you are thoughtful and honest you will always be seen in a positive manner.

Divination Considerations

As I have said previously, divination is very important because it lets you know what is happening with your magical working, both before you perform it and afterward. It is critically important that you have a competent ability to read the tarot or rune stones. I prefer tarot because there are more possible combinations, but any kind of complex divination system will help you understand the greater implications of your magical workings and your overall fate. Divination is a fluid and flexible way of looking at possible outcomes or potential futures, and it can also help you more clearly understand your own past and present.

However, the most direct and efficient system of divination are dice. I always keep a pair of dice handy in my temple and so should you. I like the outsized dice because they are easier to use and can be rolled on the temple floor without the fear of losing them. Two dice are good, but three is optimal. You can choose different colors or you can get a set of plastic knucklebones based on the oldest variation of dice.

As mentioned previously, a single die can give a "yes" or "no" answer to a quick question. A number from 1 to 2 is a negative answer, 3 to 4, neutral, and 5 and 6 is a positive answer. Usually, if you are in a situation where the summoned spirit is incommunicado, then using a single die to get yes or no answers should suffice. However, if you want to use the dice to get more involved answers to questions, you can assign specific qualities to the numbers and read them like a standard divination. The reason for doing this is to help you determine the nature or attributes of the spirit when you are unable to communicate with it. Of course, you would have to ask yes or no questions as to which attributes to check— elemental, planetary, or astrological.

One die has the possibilities of producing the numbers 1 to 6 for any given throw. Those numbers can be given the attributes of the four elements and the masculine and feminine spirit. This is how it would work.

1 = Fire, 2 = Water, 3 = Air, 4 = Earth, 5 = Feminine spirit, 6 = Masculine spirit

Example: You ask the spirit to define its quality or basic element attribute. The answer to this question would be one of the four elements, or feminine/masculine spirit.

Two dice together have the possibilities of producing the numbers 2 to 12 for any given throw. There are eleven total numbers that could be divided into 7 + 4—the seven planets and four elements.

2 = Fire, 3 = Water, 4 = Air, 5 = Earth, 6 = Sun, 7 = Moon, 8 = Mercury, 9 = Mars, 10 = Jupiter, 11 = Saturn, 12 = Venus

Example: You ask the spirit to define its quality or basic planetary attribute. If the dice throw gave the number 12 (boxcars—also known as the Venus throw), then the spirit would be associated with the attributes of love, romance, and sex. If another throw got the number 2 (snake eyes) then the second attribute would be fire. Venus and fire would be quite a passion-inducing spirit attribute combination—handle with care!

Three dice have the possibilities of producing numbers 3 to 18 for any given throw. There are 16 total numbers, so that could be divided into 12 + 4 or the twelve signs of the zodiac and four elements as seasons. You can ask questions using three dice about the specific astrological personality of the spirit to retrieve any answer that can be couched in zodiacal attributes, or you can determine the time of the year when the spirit's power is greatest.

3 = Fire–summer, 4 = Water–spring, 5 = Air–autumn,
6 = Earth–winter, 7 = Aries, 8 = Taurus, 9 = Gemini,
10 = Cancer, 11 = Leo, 12 = Virgo, 13 = Libra, 14 = Scorpio,
15 = Sagittarius, 16 = Capricorn, 17 = Aquarius, 18 = Pisces

Dice can be used in a number of different ways, but I find myself using them more often for quick answers to yes or no questions. I have found that a single die can help you make a determination when engaging a spirit. Sometimes for whatever mysterious reason, you will have to resort to using a die to help you get an answer from a spirit. I have found it to be an unfailing means of getting an answer when one is not forthcoming. So, keep your dice handy whenever you are engaging with spirits.

Exploring and Identifying Spirit World Topology

While you are invoking and evoking spirits, you can also begin to explore the spirit world that exists superimposed over your normal mundane world. To do this will require you to develop the ability to "see" the features, contours, and topology of the spirit world. You will of course be exploring that world as it exists in your local area. So if you want to explore other areas of that world, you will have to learn a few additional skills. You will have to learn to scry with a black mirror or crystal ball or travel in spirit vision, which is also known as astral projection. We will be talking more about these two skills later in this section.

Exploring your local area of the spirit world requires that you first adopt a mild trance and then travel around and explore your home and neighborhood. I call this trance walking, and it allows you to look, explore, and observe without being too obvious. While trance walking, it is important to be in a light trance and to make certain that you are not drawn into a heavier trance state, especially if you are walking around outside. While doing this exercise, you want to be able to proceed without running into or tripping over things. You might also want to keep a note-pad or digital voice recorder to take notes of what you see and observe.

If you have built up an ability to quickly enter into and out of a light trance state or that you can see the spirit world unaided, then this kind of exploration will be easy to employ and also quite fruitful. What I do to help me see into the spirit world in daylight is to close my eyes to slits in order to dim the overall input of light. Using this technique allows me to momentarily "look" into the domain of spirits whenever I wish without having to adopt a light trance. During the night it is much easier for me to see the underlying domain of spirit wherever I am, as long as the lighting is dim or if it is dark punctuated with some light. Moonlight from a full moon produces the perfect spectral illumination for seeing the spirit world while walking around outside.

Why anyone would go to the trouble of doing all of this odd spelunk-ing of the spirit world? What can be gained by knowing what the local spirit world looks like? If you are a Witch conjuror then you need to know about the world where the spirits reside in order to understand them.

The spirit world is a vast treasure house of archetypes, symbols, signs, words, and archetypal processes that have a profound impact on the world in which we live. Learning to see and perceive this world lo-cally will help you to understand how it functions and determine its features on a global level. Human beings have expressed this knowl-edge of the spirit world in theology, myths, fairy tales, and the themes and tropes of fictional stories and even in TV shows and movies. Our culture and language have their source in the local and regional spirit world, so understanding this inner and symbolic world will also help us understand ourselves and the material world in which we live. Ad-ditionally, the local world of spirits also has a lot of signs and portends about the future as well as hidden secrets of the past—all of these are available to the Witch who spends time delving into and studying them.

As I have said previously, trance states are the key to unlocking your sensory perception of the spirit world, and this is also true about the skills needed to master scrying and traveling in spirit vision. Using these techniques will assist you in being able to explore the larger domains of the spirit world, such as those that are regional and also global.

First of all, it is important to have either a question or a specific topic or theme to focus on. It could be anything, because everything has a counterpart in the world of spirit. However, I would advise you to select something that obviously has its origin in the spirit world, such as a myth, fairytale, or some local folktale. You can also pose your investigation in such a manner that you can find the archetypal or common folk sources of this theme. However, your search in the world of spirits is always precipitated by a question. Having that firmly in mind, or even going so far as writing it down, you can begin the process of investigation.

Scrying is a simple process where you stare at a crystal ball or a black mirror and then go into a deep trance and record what you see. To aid this exercise, it is helpful to allow your imagination to be fully engaged so that you will see the surface of the crystal or mirror cloud over or become opaque, and it is upon that visual surface that you will project the images of whatever is in your mind. This exercise will require a fair amount of practice, and initially you will likely see jumbled images and visual distortions that won't make much sense. After a while, as you discipline your mind, you will begin to see actual cogent visual images that may either literally or symbolically tell you a story or give you an answer. It is important to keep the question or topic firmly in your mind as you allow your eyes to gaze into the crystal or mirror and see whatever presents itself.

I would recommend that you record what you are seeing in a digital voice recorder so you can review what you saw later, and if it is valuable, write it up in your magical diary. Whenever you perform any kind of divination you should keep a blank book or notebook to write down what you experienced along with the date and the time. Keeping good notes will help you piece together seemingly disassociated or disjointed occurrences and discover the thread of continuity that pulls them together. Often I have found that such threads are even more important than the actual readings or scrying sessions.

As you scry and explore the world of spirits, it is important to remember that the world you are observing and experiencing is mostly symbolic. Whatever you realize or discover will have symbolic and even psychological ramifications. One of the most important concepts about this world is that thoughts can become form, and form can dissolve back into thoughts. What is seen or communicated in this world is often hidden or obscured by psychological symbols.

You will find living archetypes, analogies, word associations, and the whole collective cultural consciousness residing in this world.[44] To make sense of it you will need to do some research, and sometimes it will be extensive.

I typically use books that are dictionaries of signs and symbols as well as philosophic dictionaries to research puzzling things seen or heard in the spirit world. I have found that some of Carl Jung's books can help with this task as well.[45] However, what you are seeing and experiencing is being perceived and interpreted by you, so many times the answers that you are seeking are buried in your own mind. You just need to use meditation techniques to unlock them. Also, your familiar spirit can help you when you encounter something that cannot be translated or interpreted through research.

---

44 I use the term *collective consciousness* to represent the cultural and linguistic world that we live in as opposed to what Jung and other psychologists called the collective unconsciousness. Although this term is also Jungian, I don't subscribe to the concept of the unconsciousness that he and other Freudians proposed.

45 I would recommend the book *Man and His Symbols* by C. G. Jung. It is a synopsis of all of Jung's studies in psychological symbology.

Traveling in spirit vision is a different technique, and also one that is more difficult to master. The way to achieve this state is to lie down or sit in a very comfortable chair and then proceed to go into the deepest trance state that you can achieve. You need to do this without falling asleep. Instead, while in this deep trance you should try to wake your mind up to full alertness while allowing your body to remain in that deep trance state. It probably sounds kind of tricky, but it can be done with practice. One way to help you achieve this state is to use visual cues and your imagination to visualize your body going deep into trance while you seek to rouse your astral double and move it out of your body so it is standing on the floor nearby.

While going into this state, you will feel your body start to tingle (like your arm or leg does when it "goes to sleep"). Then your body will feel cool and stiff, and you will have a sensation of movement or buoyancy within the "husk" of your body. You might also briefly feel the sensations of ascending or falling. At this point of wakefulness in your mind, you only need to will your spirit body to float above and detach itself from your physical body, locked in the torpor of trance. Once you are free, you can begin to reconnoiter your surrounding area and explore it. I would do this several times just to get a knack of traveling in spirit vision and get over the distractions of your local area. Of course, when you actually do this technique to learn or observe something, you will seek to ignore the distractions around you and focus instead on the topic that you want to know. In spirit vision, you will be able to do quite a number of remarkable things like fly through the sky and travel far distances. You will have access to the whole of the spirit world and be able to not only see and hear all of the associated phenomena of this world, but you will be able to meet and talk to every kind of spirit as well.

Regaining consciousness from traveling in spirit vision requires no more ability than simply willing yourself to be rejoined with your body. If you happen to be in some distant area, just thinking of going home will bring you back to your body. Rejoining your body will wake you up, but you will definitely need to ground yourself afterward, perhaps even massaging your arms and legs to speed that process. You will feel very stiff and fuzzy headed as if you had awakened from a deep sleep but that will quickly pass. Once returned, you should immediately record what you saw and experienced in the spirit world before you forget important details. Later on you can formally write or type up what you experienced for your diary.

Another way you can "dress up" your spirit world exploration is to set up a vortex and open up the western gateway. In this magically charged environment you can scry, travel by spirit vision, or meditate to explore the more distant regional and global domains of the world of spirits. Then when you are done, you can close the gateway and seal the underlying vortex and then perform a grounding exercise. The combination of vortex and western gateway opens your conscious mind to any part of the spirit world, since what you are erecting would be considered a symbolic representation of whole world in your temple. Some have called this combination of ritual and spirit traveling a *vision quest*, since it is one way of ensuring complete immersion into wherever you go and whatever you encounter.

As you explore the world of spirit in your local area outside your home, you can pick up objects (such as a pebble, flower, or other artifact) while in the light trance state of spirit traveling and perceiving, and these objects will be imbued with the "energies" of both the mundane and spirit worlds. If such objects are selected near some large edifice or topical feature, such as a great tree, wooded glen, a park, a forgotten road, or an unusual building, they can automatically represent that feature when you take possession of them. Such artifacts of your spirit travels can be carefully selected and placed on your shrine, representing a connection to the outdoor domain of the world of spirits. By selecting artifacts from specific and striking features in the topology of the spirit world and arranging them on your shrine, you can create a kind of spider's web of connections that joins the world of spirit magically to your shrine.

You can also create artifacts by taking some small object like a coin or small pebble, consecrating it in your circle, and then hiding it near the topological object in your spirit travels. You should make two of them and join them magically by association and then take one of them and plant it in the desired location. Over time such activity will produce a powerful web that will anchor your magic to both the material and spiritual worlds and extend your direct influence throughout this area. This will assist you to sense things both of the past and the future as well as giving you a powerful material edge. Like the strands of a web to the spider in its center, nothing will occur in your area without you being sensitively aware of it.

All of these activities of spirit traveling throughout your local area and also to the farther and more archetypal regions will gradually increase your knowledge of the spirit world. I would recommend that you take these various sightings and experiences and seek to merge them into some kind of creative design or map. You will be able to build on your knowledge of the world of spirits that would include its local, regional and global topology as well as the various spirits that populate it. Not only should you learn all that you can about this world, but you should also perform formal invocations and evocations to engage with the spirits collected at various points in this topology.

Imagine this project of mapping the spirit world being like what you would do if you had just moved to a new neighborhood and a new home. You would want to explore the area and get to know your neighbors. You might even want to know the best places to go for information, assistance, or just plain local gossip. Having an entirely new and strange world open up to you is a lot like moving to a new neighborhood. Of course, the differences are that you have to learn to see, hear and understand this world, and it is a lot more subtle than the material world you are used to engaging with. However, the knowledge and the contacts that you will gain will greatly help you be a wiser and more capable Witch, and that is the whole point to taking on this kind of work.

Your preeminent guide to the world of spirits and the entities that populate it is your personal Godhead, higher self, or familiar spirit. This intimate deity is your helper, assistant, guide, and guardian. Whatever gaps or omissions you might encounter in your knowledge, research, or even magical ability will be filled and smoothed over by this ever-vigilant helper. Your personal Godhead will assist you in deciphering any obscure symbol, translating spirit languages you might encounter, and helping to manage and control the various spirits that you will either invoke or evoke. Of course it is important for you to maintain that relationship, and you should regularly commune and open yourself completely to this benign entity, maintaining a kind of dialogue. Since your personal deity is actually a manifestation of your true self as a god, you couldn't find a closer companion or more faithful helper if you tried. Soul mates can't even hold a candle to your personal Godhead, so this is one relationship that you should do everything possible to keep intact and fully active. The personal Godhead is the first entity installed in your shrine, and that is the best place for it to reside, since the shrine is central to all of your spiritual and magical activity.

The world of spirit is all around you, but the hub of that world is your shrine. It is the axis mundi of everything that you will do; from your spiritual alignments and liturgical obligations to the exploration of the various geographic and symbolic places, and the whole of the spirit hosts found therein. This whole universe of spiritual and material worlds that exists in one space and one place is controlled and subject to your shrine, developed and built up by you over a period of years of magical workings. It is the ultimate boon and the greatest tool that a Witch conjuror can possess, but it has to be carefully assembled, nurtured, amplified, and kept active in order to achieve the highest objective—mastery of the spirit world. That is the ultimate objective, of course, and it is one the great witches of antiquity were reputed to have achieved.

Included with the shrine is also the black Book of Spirits, or *Liber Sprituum*, where you will put all of the material you have assembled for each of the spirits that you have invoked or evoked. This includes the consecrated sigil and the diary entries for the time and date when the spirit was summoned. The pact should also be included along with some notes about the outcome and whether it was successful or not. In some cases, there might be more than one pact if a spirit proved itself able and helpful in achieving objectives.

The Book of Spirits is also an active and accumulative magical tool, since all the Witch conjuror has to do to call a spirit that was once summoned is to open the book, light a candle and ring a bell, or some such combination. Performing some kind of simple recall spell will cause the spirit to reappear. Such a simple kind of rite is, of course, an informal summoning. Yet because it was formally summoned at a previous time, it is a stronger and more potent manifestation than just an informal summoning alone would be. I would recommend keeping the Book of Spirits on the shrine if that can be done without it enticing someone to examine it. You can also use a book that has locking straps to keep unwanted folks from opening it up. Because it is a magical artifact, it should be kept discreetly and away from anyone's nosey intrusion, since merely opening and reading it will have a magical effect, however great or small.

We have now covered all the material you will need to know to be a Witch conjuror. However, you should also be aware that there is a lot of material available for you to explore and use as you see fit. The difference is that you now have a complete system of conjuring magic based on your tradition of Witchcraft or Paganism. You won't have to adopt any of the old grimoires as your foundational practice because you already have a foundational practice. What you can do is research these other works and appropriate whatever you find that is relevant or appealing.

All of this research activity is optional, so I put together a list for you to examine in Appendix Two. The books listed in the appendix are for your enrichment should you decide to explore this topic more thoroughly.

–Epilogue–
Spirit Conjuring and the Spirit Traveling Witch

We are not human beings on a spiritual journey.
We are spiritual beings on a human journey.

STEPHEN R. COVEY

We began this book with the premise that the art of formally summoning spirits was somehow missing from the various Witchcraft and Pagan traditions. That the basic convenstead magic circle protected the individuals within it from any contact with the spirit world
except what was sanctioned by their tradition. This was despite the fact
that the magic circle was really a boundary between the material and
spiritual worlds, and that Witches were standing on the threshold of the
Spirit World but not really stepping fully into it. Therefore, in order for
Witches and Pagans to be able to fully enter that world and to engage with
it at local, regional, and global levels they had to adopt some new rites and
extend their existing lore. This was the approach advocated in the beginning of this work, and I believe I have fulfilled my objective through the
contents of this book.

What I did was add the simple rituals for godhead assumption, the Rose Ankh vortex, and the western gateway to establish the proper magical and liturgical environment for conjuring spirits. I also added three or five steps that one would follow to either invoke or evoke a spirit. Additionally, there are the tools of the shrine and the Book of Spirits (*Liber Spirituum*) that represent the source and the record of all of the spiritual alignments and the achievements for summoning spirits. I have also emphasized the need for the Witch to be more involved with their spirituality and make not only offerings and devotions to their personal godhead but also to other spirits that by necessity had become part of their spiritual alliance.

I have also discussed that the Witch should establish an intimate knowledge of their local area from the standpoint of the spirit world and that they discover and engage with the local spirits and deities in that environment. All of these efforts will foster a completely different kind of Witch or Pagan once they are followed for a period of time. I envision that this new discipline will produce individuals who are faithfully functioning within the spirit theory of magic. It is my opinion that too many Witches and Pagans omit this approach to both their liturgical workings and magical experiments.

This book has presented a methodology that has taken the work out of the coven or grove group context and placed it back into the hands of the individual. While spirit conjuring can be done in a group setting, it is mostly a singular and solo operation. In antiquity, a Witch was a lone figure who worked her magic in complete privacy, and the only exception was when she had a paying client. A coven or grove can take the pressure off of an individual since liturgical rites and magic are performed by a group led by a competent leader or a small group of knowledgeable elders.

In the method I have proposed, all of this work is assumed by the individual since it must primarily focus on the individual deity that lies within each person. Because the personal deity is the guardian and guide assumed by the Witch, and because the Witch must build and develop this relationship over time, there seems to be little opportunity for spirit summoning to be a group activity. It appears to me that group activity would be limited to one Witch doing the work and the others would simply observe. However, it has always been the responsibility for the individual to pursue a path of occult education and magical expertise that can only be gained by solitary work. For those who are so inclined to master their craft, I have written and dedicated this book.

Some individuals might have a problem with what I am promoting because it would appear to weaken the coven or grove group structure and place more emphasis on the individual. However, I believe this perception is erroneous for three reasons: it never hurts a group to have the individual members become more experienced and knowledgeable, because a group is only as strong as its weakest link.

It would also help the group become more engaged with their deities and more inclined to make offerings and devotions, since it would be a feature in their individual practice. And it would break up the hierarchy of leaders and make everyone more equal and capable of sharing leadership positions—taking pressure off of the leaders.

Perhaps it is the third reason that some leaders and elite members of a group would find a problem with what I am proposing. This is because their members would no longer be dependent on them, and the power structure they represent would have to be moderated lest the group splinter.

Since I have a problem with static group hierarchies in the first place, I would be a strong advocate for individual empowerment and responsibility. That fact alone might make me some enemies in the community, but a wise leader knows that a position of authority is temporary and only exists by the grace and acceptance of the group. A group consisting of equals is always healthy, as opposed to one ruled by one or a few. If adopting my methods of conjuring ends up breaking up some tyrannical groups, I'll consider it a bonus.

I have also discussed in detail how you can take your current practices and tradition and add to it the ability to conjure spirits and engage fully with the spirit world. What I have outlined is a complete tradition and a practical system of magic by itself. This tradition of spirit conjuration is one that should be an integral part of any Witchcraft or Pagan system of magic. It also represents that spirit work is an important addition to the established domain of modern Witchcraft and Paganism.

If enough people take on the work proposed in this book (or some variation of it) and it becomes a core part of practical magic and religious practices, I think that these religious traditions will become more like their distant relatives in antiquity. This will have a kind of "darkening" effect on these traditions, and some people will have no problem with engaging and even worshiping the chthonic aspects of their deities and all that such an alignment encompasses. I expect that demonolatry will become more popular than it is now for individuals practicing Witchcraft and Paganism. I don't have a problem with that bias, since it has apparently produced some very excellent cutting-edge magical works and experiments, and it has released some people from pretending to be harmless workers of white light-only magic.

While I have tried to cover everything that I could in a book of this size, some of you may feel that what I have written isn't enough for you to make the transition to become a spirit conjuror. If you feel that I have gone over the rituals for godhead assumption, the Rose Ankh vortex, and the western gateway all too briefly, then I can at least suggest some other sources that go into these rituals in a more in-depth manner. These sources are works I wrote, so I can at least attest that they deal thoroughly with these three rituals. *Mastering the Art of Ritual Magick*, omnibus edition (Megalithica, 2010) contains separate chapters that not only go over these rituals, but also shows you how to rewrite them into your own tradition. You can find the rituals in Book II of this single edition work located in chapters 9, 10, and 11. The directions for re-writing these rituals can be found in Book III, located in chapter 5.

I would like to end this work with a cautionary tale full of folly and youthful hubris. You see, I was a teenage Witch, but that was before I was properly initiated and taught how to work magic in the Alexandrian tradition. I was also young, hardly eighteen years old, and learning to function as a Witch in a small Midwestern town.

My friends and I sought to pierce that veil between worlds and somehow gain miraculous powers in the material world aided by the spirit world. I now know that this is an impossible feat, but such things seemed quite possible when I was an overly imaginative youth. This was an important object lesson for me. I can tell you the tale so you will be able to use your critical thinking skills and not fall prey to motivational reasoning, which seems so rife in our political culture today.

My tale is taken from one of my blog articles, "Tales of Wisdom and Folly."[46]

One episode that sticks in my mind happened in a place where we would go for an adventure while in the highly suggestive and altered state of intoxication. We would get really stoned and pile into my friend Bob's car, and he would drive off to some weird part of town he had checked out previously. We would get out and explore it as if we were in another reality altogether, which in a manner, we were.

Our favorite place was a drainage ravine, oddly, as we thought it was very magical. It ran through an old neighborhood down so low and heavily wooded that it was completely obscured even in the middle of winter. I think this was off of Spring Street near Lincoln and Horlick parks. The Root River runs through that area and even splits off to form two separate rivers; this valley was probably part of a natural drainage area. No houses were built down there, of course, but houses lined either side of the gorge,

---

46 I have edited the original so that it is more grammatically correct and readable.

which was probably thirty to forty feet high. The area of the gorge was heavily wooded and filled with undergrowth, but a small creek wended its way through the center of the valley where no trees or undergrowth grew. It was like a fairy den or a ghost road sequestered in the middle of the town's residential area.

We often went down to that place to explore and hang out—we could walk for a few miles uninterrupted along this ravine. It was accessed from a children's playground (where our adventure started), but we would climb a fence and carefully follow a pathway down into our secret magic grotto.

I recall specifically one time we were down there, quite smashed and experimenting with extracting magical power from that place, when I began to summon a great power into myself, using a combination of potent-sounding nonsense words of power mixed with some Enochian. It was a spontaneous occurrence, but I remember feeling the power fill my body and soul.

My friends joined in this activity with me, and I believe they felt the same thing. Then I said to them, "*Run with the power and let it lift you and fly!*" So we all started running along the creek with me in the lead. More swiftly and rapidly down the narrow corridor of the valley we flew. I felt as if I was about to get airborne, as if the wind that was blowing against my back was about to take us all into the air. Suddenly, I tripped and fell face first into the mud. My friends also fell, probably tripped up by me, and we were all piled together in the mud and the water of that tiny stream. Thankfully it was winter, so much of the mud and water was frozen into ice, but it made the fall more harsh and painful.

Once I had caught my breath, I started to laugh out loud, but I really wanted to cry because I had failed to fly through the air. I had felt I was so close; it was so frustrating! I wrote it off as just a test of our abilities, but it was a clear sign we were too much into our imaginations and nearly delusional in our relation to the real world. I have carried this memory with me to this day. I had not flown into the air—instead I crashed into the mud like an idiot. It was a sign of what was soon to pass in my real life.

Youthful exuberance cannot in any way violate physical laws. There are limitations, and even magic must obey them to some extent. If you have an encounter with a spirit and it tells you that it can make you fly in the air, miraculously transport you from one location to another, transmute lead into gold, or any other seemingly impossible task, you should take what it says with a grain of salt. Often what spirits say to us are analogies or parables we have to interpret but should not take literally.

We should also be cautious in accepting things the spirits tell us (and even our friends). Generally, we should be skeptical but open-minded. The worst thing anyone can do is to take everything encountered in the spirit world literally. It is also important to understand that our world has material-based limitations. While it might be remotely possible for someone to purchase a winning lottery ticket through the aid of magic, it is far less likely that someone can make a celebrity fall in love with them from a distance without any kind of social connection. That is the lesson I learned so many years ago, and it was reinforced by other minor youthful disappointments and discouragements. I had a lot to learn back then, and I suppose everyone has to learn these lessons in some manner.

What I hope is that by presenting this humorous tale, maybe you will be spared this kind of folly. The comical event shows that real magical occurrences are very much a part of our normal existence and life's lessons. Movies like *The Craft* only show that magic is easy and effortless if not without moral consequences; the truth is that magic is hard, it requires a great deal of work, and it still doesn't always produce glamorous and fantastic results.

As a final note, I would like to give you the web address for my blog. There are hundreds of articles already out there mostly indexed by subject on the left-bottom side of the web page panel. I have written articles about nearly every subject in the area of Witchcraft and Ritual Magic you might find interesting or useful. The address is: fraterbarrabbas .blogspot.com, and I hope you visit from time to time to read all of the articles I have posted there.

May the gods and goddesses of all pantheons bless and keep you well.

Frater Barrabbas

–Appendix One–
Spirit Lists: Detailed Category of Various Angels and Demons

Here are the lists of the various spirits I have collected from a number of sources and use in my own workings. In many cases I have preserved the actual original language (in this case the Hebrew letters) to work out the spelling I use. The letter combination "a'a" represents the letter *aiyin*, but the rest I have kept as simple as possible so you could make sigils from any of these names using either the Hebrew alphabet wheel or the English one. There are twelve lists displayed, and each was taken from specific sources I have already discussed previously.

Super Archangels, Archangels, Choir of Angels, and Goetic Demons

There are quite a number of variations in the lists of super archangels and archangels, not to mention the choirs of angels. I have derived my own list for the super archangels, but the archangels are taken from the

Qabalistic tradition. I would recommend checking over the Appendix section of *A Dictionary of Angels*, most notably from pages 336 through 339 and 342 so you can see how I was able to derive these names. These lists can also be found in *777* and *The Complete Magician's Tables*; there is an index for spirit names in the latter book but not in the former.

Keep in mind that these higher level celestial emissaries are effective in revealing higher forms of spiritual knowledge (gnosis), inspiring, illuminating, giving spiritual healing, protecting from evil, giving prophetic visions and insights, and assisting in mediating the higher aspects of the godhead (as the unified spirit or one).

Seraphim
(Throne Angels—can be associated with the four elements)
Metatron: Fire
Seraphiel: Water
Uriel: Air
Yahoel: Earth

Cherubim
(Guardian Angels—can be associated with the four elements)
Kerubiel: Fire
Ophaniel: Water
Rikbiel: Air
Zahariel: Earth

Archangels
(Greater Emissaries—can be associated with the ten Sephiroth)
Metatron: Kether
Ratziel: Chokmah
Tzaphqiel: Binah
Tzadqiel: Chesed

Ariel: Geburah
Raphael: Tiphareth
Haniel: Netzach
Michael: Hod
Gabriel: Yesod
Sandalphon: Malkuth

Choirs of Angels

(Lesser Emissaries—can be associated with the Ten Sephiroth)
Hayoth Haqadesh (Holy Living Things): Kether
Auphanim (Wheels of Fire): Chokmah
Arelim (Valiant Ones): Binah
Chasmalim (Brilliant Ones): Chesed
Tarshishim (Shining Ones): Geburah
Malakim (Kings): Tiphareth
Elohim (Gods): Netzach
Beni Elohim (Sons of God): Hod
Elim (Mighty Ones): Yesod
Ishim (Illuminated Men): Malkuth

12 Zodiacal Archangels & Angels

(Zodiacal Greater and Lesser Emissaries)
The archangel is the ruler of the sign, and the angel is the servitor. Higher intelligence attributes of the zodiacal sign would go with the ruler, and material attributes would be associated with the servitor.

Aries: Malchidiel or Sarahiel
Taurus: Asmodiel or Araziel
Gemini: Ambriel or Saraiel
Cancer: Muriel or Phakiel/Rahdar
Leo: Varchiel or Shartiel

Virgo: Hamaliel or Shaltiel
Libra: Zoriel or Chadaqie
Scorpio: Zuriel or Hadakiel
Sagittarius: Barbiel or Saissaiel
Capricorn: Adnachiel or Saritaiel/Vhnori
Aquarius: Hanael or Semaqiel
Pisces: Barakiel or Vacabiel/Rasamasa

36 Angels of the Decans [47]

The angels of the decans are the rulers of zodiacal demarcations consisting of ten-degree sections of the 360-degree circle of the zodiac. There are a number of associations for decans, and one of them is the 36 lesser arcana cards of the tarot numbers 2 to 10 for the four suits. Along with the tarot cards are the planetary aspects associated with both the decan and the lesser arcana tarot. The decans are also the rulers of the smaller division of the zodiac, called the quinians, which are five-degree sections. What this means is that the angelic rulers of the decans are also the rulers of the Ha-Shem angels and the Goetic demons. The key to the whole structure of the decans and their meanings are found in the naib cards of the tarot. (Alphabetic order with attributes)

Abdaron: (6 of Swords) Mercury in Aquarius (10–20°)
Abuha: (10 of Wands) Saturn in Sagittarius (20–30°)
Alinkayer: (4 of Cups) Moon in Cancer (20–30°)
Ananaurah: (8 of Disks) Sun in Virgo (0–10°)
Auron: (9 of Cups) Jupiter in Pisces (10–20°)

---

47 See Aleister Crowley, *777 and Other Qabalistic Writings* (York Beach, ME: Weiser, 1994) tables CXLVI–CLI for Hebrew spelling and listing by twelve zodiacal houses for ascendant, succeedant, and cadent decans and their magical images. Also, Aleister Crowley, *The Book of Thoth* (New York: Samuel Weiser, 1972), 283 for the planetary attributes of the thirty-six naibs cards of the tarot.

Bahalmi: (8 of Cups) Saturn in Pisces (0–10°)

Behhemi: (3 of Wands) Sun in Aries (10–20°)

Bithon: (10 of Wands) Sun in Gemini (20–30°)

Garodiel: (7 of Swords) Moon in Aquarius (20–30°)

Kamox: (5 of Cups) Mars in Scorpio (0–10°)

Kedamadi: (5 of Disks) Mercury in Taurus (0–10°)

Lusnahar: (5 of Wands) Saturn in Leo (0–10°)

Manacherai: (6 of Disks) Moon in Taurus (10–20°)

Masenin: (2 of Disks) Jupiter in Capricorn (0–10°)

Mashephar: (10 of Disks) Mercury in Virgo (20–30°)

Mesheret: (8 of Wands) Mercury in Sagittarius (0–10°)

Methraush: (2 of Cups) Venus in Cancer (0–10°)

Nindohar: (6 of Cups) Sun in Scorpio (10–20°)

Rahdax: (3 of Cups) Mercury in Cancer (10–20°)

Raidyah: (9 of Disks) Venus in Virgo (10–20°)

Sagaresh: (8 of Swords) Jupiter in Gemini (0–10°)

Saharnax: (3 of Swords) Saturn in Libra (10–20°)

Sahiber: (7 of Wands) Mars in Leo (20–30°)

Saspham: (5 of Swords) Venus in Aquarius (0–10°)

Sateriph: (10 of Cups) Mars in Pisces (20–30°)

Setneder: (4 of Wands) Venus in Aries (20–30°)

Shachdar: (4 of Swords) Jupiter in Libra (20–30°)

Shahdani: (9 of Swords) Mars in Gemini (10–20°)

Taresni: (2 of Swords) Moon in Libra (0–10°)

Vaharin: (9 of Wands) Moon in Sagittarius (10–20°)

Vathrodiel: (7 of Cups) Venus in Scorpio (20–30°)

Yaksagnox: (7 of Disks) Saturn in Taurus (20–30°)

Yasandiberodiel: (4 of Disks) Sun in Capricorn (20–30°)

Yasiseyah: (3 of Disks) Mars in Capricorn (10–20°)

Zacha'ai: (6 of Wands) Jupiter in Leo (10–20°)

Zezar: (2 of Wands) Mars in Aries (0–10°)

72 Ha-Shem Angels [48]

The Ha-Shem angels are known as the angels of the Shemhamphorash. The 72 angelic names are derived from three passages in the Old Testament, where coincidentally each passage has exactly 72 characters. When the letters are stacked in a certain order, they produce 72 three-letter groupings, where adding EL or YH to the letters will produce the name of an angel. The attributes for these 72 spirits consists of the five-degree sections of the 360-degree zodiac, known as the quinians. Two quinians are under the control of one decan (denoted by a name in parenthesis below), representing the "day" and "night" division of a decan. (Alphabetic order with attributes)

A'almayah: (Zacha'ai) by night
A'amamyah: (Behhemi) by night
A'anavael: (Shahdani) by day
A'ariel: (Auron) by night
A'ashalyah: (Sateriph) by day
Akayah: (Ananaurah) by day
Aladeyah: (Raidyah) by day
Aniel: (Saspham) by day
Aya'ael: (Methraush) by day
Cha'ameyah: (Saspham) by night
Checheshyah: (Behhemi) by day
Damabyah: (Bithon) by day
Daniel: (Zezar) by night
Ha'ayah: (Mesheret) by night
Habuyah: (Methraush) by night

---

48 See Aleister Crowley, *777* tables CXXIX–CXXXII for Hebrew spellings—Ha-Shem angel pairs by day and night and associated with the 36 cards of the lesser arcana of the tarot.

Haha'ayah: (Mashephar) by night

Hahehael: (Garodiel) by day

Hahuyah: (Vathrodiel) by night

Harachael: (Yaksagnox) by day

Hariel: (Saharnax) by day

Haziel: (Raidyah) by night

Heqameyah: (Saharnax) by night

Hiyael: (Alinkayer) by day

Kaliel: (Shachdar) by night

Kohethael: (Ananaurah) by night

Kuqeyah: (Yasandiberodiel) by day

Lahachyah: (Yasiseyah) by night

Laveyah: (Shachdar) by day

Laviel: (Mashephar) by day

Lekabael: (Masenin) by day

Lelahael: (Sahiber) by night

Lovayah: (Kamox) by day

Mabahael: (Taresni) by night

Mabaheyah: (Kedamadi) by day

Machiel: (Shahdani) by night

Mahashyah: (Sahiber) by day

Malahael: (Vathrodiel) by day

Manadael: (Yasandiberodiel) by night

Manaqael: (Bithon) by night

Maxerael: (Yaksagnox) by night

Meyakael: (Garodiel) by night

Mihael: (Sateriph) by night

Mumayah: (Alinkayer) by night

Nalakael: (Nindohar) by day

Namameyah: (Manacherai) by day

Nanael: (Setneder) by day
Nithael: (Setneder) by night
Nithhayah: (Mesheret) by day
Omael: (Abuha) by night
Phahaleyah: (Kamox) by night
Poyael: (Kedamadi) by night
Raha'ael: (Abdaron) by day
Rahael: (Rahdax) by day
Riyael: (Abuha) by day
Sahiyah: (Vaharin) by night
Saleyah: (Auron) by day
Sitael: (Zacha'ai) by day
Vahuel: (Zezar) by day
Vahuyah: (Lusnahar) by day
Vemabael: (Sagaresh) by day
Vesharyah: (Masenin) by night
Vuleyah: (Bahalmi) by day
Yabmeyah: (Rahdax) by night
Yahahael: (Sagaresh) by night
Yarethael: (Vaharin) by day
Yechuyah: (Yasiseyah) by day
Yelaheyah: (Bahalmi) by night
Yeliel: (Lusnahar) by night
Yezalael: (Taresni) by day
Yilael: (Manacherai) by night
Yiyael: (Nindohar) by night
Yizael: (Abdaron) by night

72 Goetic Spirits[49]

Goetic spirits represent the classic names of demons that have come down to us from antiquity, although it is a list that grew and evolved over time. The earliest variations of this list contained a few dozen of the spirit names that we would recognize today, and over time additional names were added to it. The definitive spirit list, from the sixteenth century, can be found in the manuscripts of the *Grimoirum Verum* (*True Grimoire*), where there are around 69 demons. The *Goetia*, which was the first volume of the *Lemegeton* or *Lesser Key of Solomon* is a later version that has 72 demons. The transit of this material from the *True Grimoire* to the *Goetia* ended up losing one demon (Pruslas) and adding four more names to the list. In my list I have added the missing demon from the *True Grimoire* to the list of 72, making 73.

However, the 72 demons could also be associated with the 72 quinians of the 360 degrees of the zodiac, as are the Ha-Shem angels. While this appears to make a tight corresponding system it might also be too convenient and contrived. However, the 22 trumps of the tarot is based on a contrived number as well, but it works extremely well. The characters or seals for evoking the 72 Goetic demons are to be found in the *Lemegeton* volume of the *Goetia*.[50] I have associated each of these spirits with the angel ruler of the decan whose name is in parenthesis. (Alphabetic order with attributes)

Ager: (Behhemi) by day
Aligosh: (Sahiber) by day
Alok: (Ananaurah) by night
Amedok: (Saspham) by night

---

49   Aleister Crowley, *777*, tables CLV–CLX.
50   Joseph H. Peterson, *The Lesser Key of Solomon* (York Beach, ME: Weiser, 2001), 7–39.

Amon: (Sagaresh) by day

Andar: (Abuha) by night

Andaraleph: (Yasiseyah) by night

Andromal: (Sateriph) by night

Ashteroth: (Yasiseyah) by day

Asmodai: (Abdaron) by day

Avael: (Rahdax) by night

Avan: (Kamox) by night

Ayem: (Nindohar) by day

Ba'alem: (Sahiber) by night

Baleth: (Lusnahar) by day

Baliel: (Abdaron) by night

Barbetosh: (Shahdani) by day

Bathin: (Mashephar) by day

Bayem: (Vaharin) by day

Bel: (Zezar) by day

Berith: (Masenin) by day

Bipharo: (Methraush) by night

Botish: (Raidyah) by day

Buar: (Methraush) by day

Danamael: (Auron) by night

Dekorab: (Garodiel) by night

Gamigin: (Kedamadi) by day

Gexaph: (Garodiel) by day

Glaslabul: (Mesheret) by day

Gosyon: (Rahdax) by day

Ha'agnath: (Alinkayer) by night

Haleph: (Behhemi) by night

Haur: (Masenin) by night

Kain: (Raidyah) by night

Karokal: (Lusnahar) by night
Kimaur: (Yasandiberodiel) by night
Laraik: (Zacha'ai) by day
Maleph: (Setneder) by night
Marax: (Shachdar) by day
Marchosh: (Auron) by day
Mareb: (Manacherai) by day
Morem: (Mashephar) by night
Namor: (Saharnax) by night
Neber: (Vathrodiel) by day
Nephol: (Vathrodiel) by night
Oriax: (Nindohar) by night
Orob: (Taresni) by night
Phaimeran: (Bithon) by day
Phanax: (Zezar) by night
Phok: (Zacha'ai) by night
Phukelor: (Manacherai) by night
Phurnash: (Yasandiberodiel) by day
Porphur: (Bahalmi) by day
Pruslas: N/A
Purash: (Saspham) by day
Purshon: (Saharnax) by day
Raum: (Kedamadi) by night
Rinvav: (Abuha) by day
Shabnik: (Sagaresh) by night
Shalosh: (Taresni) by day
Shar: (Bahalmi) by night
Shax: (Shahdani) by night
Shitari: (Alinkayer) by day

Vael: (Vaharin) by night
Valephar: (Yaksagnox) by day
Vashago: (Setneder) by day
Vephar: (Yaksagnox) by night
Veshav: (Shachdar) by night
Vina: (Bithon) by night
Yaphosh: (Kamox) by day
Yashtolosh: (Sateriph) by day
Zagen: (Mesheret) by night
Zapher: (Ananaurah) by day

Theurgia-Goetia

The *Theurgia-Goetia* is the second volume of the *Lemegeton* and was supposedly written by Trithemius, the teacher and mentor of Agrippa. These spirits consist of four classes that could be compared to the four elements (Emperors), sixteen elementals (Grand Dukes), forty-eight zodiacal elements (Dukes), and the twelve planetary attributes (the eleven Wandering Princes with one duplicate). The characters and seals for invoking these spirits can be found in the *Goetia of Dr. Rudd* by Stephen Skinner and David Rankin.[51] These spirits are seen as a combination of angels and demons. (Alphabetic order)

4 Emperors: Rulers
Ameradiel
Carmasiel (Carnesiel)
Caspiel
Demoriel

---

51 Skinner and Rankine, *The Goetia of Dr. Rudd,* 213–306.

16 Grand Dukes [52]

Armadiel

Aschiel

Asyriel

Barmiel

Baruchas

Cabariel

Camuel

Dorochiel

Godiel

Malgaras

Maseriel

Padiel

Pamersiel

Rasiel

Symiel

Usiel

48 Dukes

Almesiel

Ambri

Aridiel

Arifiel

Armany

Arnibiel

Balsur

Bedary

Benoliam

---

52   The sixteen elementals are the compounded elements—such as Fire of Water, Air of Earth, etc. These can also correspond to the sixteen court cards in the tarot.

Bucafas

Budarim

Burisiel

Cabarim

Camiel

Camor

Camory

Capriel

Carnol

Chamiel

Chariel

Churibal

Codriel

Curifas

Curmeriel

Dabrinos

Doriel

Dubilon

Femol

Geriel

Lamael

Laphor

Larmol

Luziel

Mador

Maras

Medar

Menador

Musiriel

Myrezyn

Nadroc

Oriel

Ornich

Rapsiel

Ursiel

Vadriel

Vadros

Zabriel

Zoeniel

11 Wandering Princes

Bidiel

Buriel

Emoniel

Geradiel

Hydriel

Icosiel

Macariel

Menadiel

Pirchiel

Soloviel

Uriel

Twenty Chiefs of the Nephilim

The Nephilim are the Fallen Angels as related in chapter 6 of the Old Testament book of Genesis, where the Sons of God came to earth to mate with the Daughters of Man. They were the spirits who taught the arts of civilization and the occult to their brides and also to their children, who were considered giants or famous men. These fallen angels had a particular reverence for humanity and represent the progressive spiritual elements operating in society that seek to free individuals from ignorance and bondage.

While these entities were vilified in the Book of Enoch, they are perhaps more relevant and to be deemed helpful to individuals seeking knowledge and self-empowerment.[53] I have extensively worked with these spirits and have found them to be universally positive and profoundly revelatory.

In the list below, four of the Nephilim are the greater chiefs (A'asael (Fire), Ramtel (Air), Shemichazah (Water), and Turiel (Earth), the rest of the sixteen spirits are loosely aligned with one greater chief or another.

This is a hierarchical structure with an element-based configuration. Further information can be found by evoking and conversing with them.

Artaqoph

Baraqel

Daniel

Hermoni

Kohabiel

Matarel

Omanel

A'asael (Asael or Azazel)

Ramael

Ramtel

Sahriel

Satavel

Shamshiel

Shemichazah

Tamiel

Tumiel

Turiel

Yehadiel

---

53   George W. E. Nickelsburg and James C. Vanderkam, *1 Enoch: A New Translation* (Minneapolis, MN: Fortress Press, 2004), 23–26.

Yomiel

Zeqiel

Infernal Hierarchy

I have also decided to include the seven infernal princes and four demon chiefs, which might be needed in order to fully establish a system of demonolatry. I removed Asmodeus from the list of princes because he is also included in the list of 72 Goetic demons (as Asmodai). The list of four chiefs and their governors represent the root of the hierarchy for the 72 demons who would be placed under one of these (4 x 18) chiefs. (I have derived this list from a number of traditional sources.)

Seven Infernal Princes

Lucifer

Mammon

Leviathan

Beelzebub

Amon

Satan

Belphegor

Four Demon Chiefs and their Governors

Uriens/Oriens: Thelfryon

Amaymon: Boytheon

Paymon: Sperion

Egin: Mayerion

–Appendix Two–
Overview of the Old Grimoires
and How to Use Them

This appendix contains some basic considerations as to what are the old grimoires: Where did they come from? When? Why are they important today? Speaking generally, a grimoire is a book of rituals, spells, spirit lists, characters or seals, and other regalia for magical protection, containment, and empowerment.

There are modern books of rituals and spells available in nearly every bookstore (except a religious one of course), but these books are special because they come from source manuscripts that are centuries old. Even the Book of Shadows can be considered a kind of grimoire, since the modern traditions of Witchcraft are not religious traditions that have sacred scriptures. The difference is that the Book of Shadows is a modern grimoire and the old classic grimoires have a verifiable historical pedigree.

The old grimoires of popular imagination come down to us mostly from Renaissance Europe and were usually written in Latin, but later versions were transcribed into the vernacular of the region where they were used. Older books from the Middle Ages and early Renaissance certainly did exist, representing the earliest renditions of these works. Yet much of this material was appropriated into the later classic grimoires. Thus there was a kind of appropriation process of borrowing that binds these books together from the earliest period to the latest.

There is much speculation about where these books ultimately had their origin and there appears to be some evidence that the classic grimoires came from Constantinople, functioning as a crossroads for Western Europe and the Middle East. This great city was also the font and archive of the last vestiges of antiquity, so it likely had quite a cache of occult and magical literature. Once the Turks conquered Constantinople in the middle of the fifteenth century, many books, including the hermetic writings of Hermes Trismegistus, were secreted out of the fallen city. From there, these books spread into Italy, Spain, and also southern France and Germany, following the same path as the spread of occult literature such as the Qabalah.

The church condemned all these books, and they were banned from even being in one's possession. It is quite fortunate for us that any of these books survived the passage of time to be available today. However, despite being banned they were also very popular, particularly in the seventeenth and eighteenth centuries, during what was called the Age of Reason. Because of their popularity and ubiquity, some manuscripts were preserved from destruction or loss to be compiled and copied during the early modern era. What we have today represents only a small percentage of the total books that once existed for the sole purpose of performing some form of magic.

The first important consideration about the old grimoires is that most of them were originally hand-written manuscripts, although there were some that were later published in special and anonymous printings. This means that there wasn't one definitive version or edition of a specific grimoire. There were in fact hundreds of different versions and some of them were completely different. As an example, there wasn't just one book called the *Greater Key of Solomon*, there were hundreds, and not all of them even had the same contents—they just happened to share the same title. Later published grimoires only aggregated various manuscripts or focused on just one and omitted others completely, making them incomplete representations of the title genre.

Another consideration is that the supposed authors of these books were completely obscured by mythic authors, such as Solomon, St. Cyprian, or even Moses. These were legendary individuals who had become associated in some way with the practice of magic. Of course, these individuals didn't write these books, so we don't know who the real authors were. These manuscripts were surreptitiously passed around amongst an elite literate group of savants and clerics. They were copied many times by many different individuals, and each book had various additions and omissions added or subtracted to each unique volume. In a sense, many hands helped to write and evolve these books over the centuries, so there wasn't really one single author. Historians have identified, in some cases, a few brilliant individuals who probably wrote the first versions, but what they wrote was then copied by others into new versions, and sometimes entirely new books. Still, these books became infamous amongst the literati of the times, and they still have an attractive patina of dark and forbidden powers to this day.

Over the last couple of decades, a concerted effort by historians has not only discovered a number of these manuscripts, but they have been translated, historically analyzed, and made available to the general reading public. When I was a young man, you could count the number of grimoires available in print on one hand. Now there are many published books and still more are being translated and published to this day. With so many to choose from, I have decided to present a dozen of these books that are the best resources available for your selection. We are so fortunate today that there is such a plethora of grimoires available to us, and we owe a debt of gratitude to those historians and also occultists who have been at the forefront of this publishing bonanza.

So, what are the most important grimoires I would actually recommend to someone? Some of these books are pricey; others are reasonable. Of course, the purpose for collecting one or more of these books is to appropriate the lore they contain. After all, that's the main purpose for which I would buy an expensive limited-edition book. It would be to add lore to my own magical work, as I am not really in the business of collecting books for their own sake.

The author Owen Davies wrote an article for *The Guardian's* online newspaper about the top ten grimoires in history.[54] This article was passed around the occult community and created quite a bit of favorable buzz. I read it and had some different ideas, but I also wanted to expand the list to twelve books as well. I would also highly recommend his book *Grimoires: A History of Magical Books* because it tells the historical story about the grimoires, where they came from, and who read and used them spanning a period of time that was over a thousand years. Mr. Davies has a much better grasp of the historical context to these books than I do. I also think these historical narratives are important to know.

According to Owen Davies' article, the top ten grimoires in his esteemed opinion are as follows: *Sixth and Seventh Books of Moses, Clavicule (Lesser Key) of Solomon, Petit Albert,* the *Book of St. Cyprian,* the *Dragon Rouge* (variation of the *Grande Grimoire*), the *(Sworn) Book of Honorius, Fourth Book of Occult Philosophy, The Magus, Necronomicon,* and the *Book of Shadows*. These might be the most popular books that have had the biggest impact on European and American cultures, but they are not the most useful books in my opinion. I would scratch the

---

54   See online link for the newspaper article—*Top 10 Grimoires* by Owen Davies: www.theguardian.com/books/2009/apr/08/history.

Necromonicon and the *Book of Shadows* off of the list to start with and then assemble, in some kind of sequence, the books that I think are the most important grimoires.

Keep in mind that these books are not exactly ordered according to their importance to me—they are all equally important. Also, there are more than one book published for each set or class of grimoires, so the actual purchasing list is greater than twelve.

Greater and Lesser Keys of Solomon—This would include the *Veritable Key of Solomon*, and the *Lemegeton*, or *Lesser Key*.

The *Greater Key of Solomon* is one of the earlier grimoires, having its source in the late thirteenth to fourteenth centuries. It may have been originally written in Constantinople and then was secreted away when that city fell to the Turks in 1455. The *Key of Solomon* mostly concerns itself with the production of planetary talismans; the preparations for conjuring spirits; and the prayers, invocations, curses, and exhortations used for them. It doesn't contain a list of spirits, but it was assumed that the spirits were hostile, such as spirits of the dead and demons. There are also quite a number of tools inscribed with a magical language. The planetary talismans and protection talismans are very popular and can be found nearly everywhere. The basis of the magic practiced in this book is Christian with Jewish magical influences.

The *Lesser Key of Solomon* is a much later addition to the Solomonic collection, being an assembly of sixteenth-century material in a book produced in the seventeenth century. The *Lesser Key* appears to add additional material that was absent from the *Greater Key*. The *Lemegeton* consists of five books, many of them appropriated from previous sources.

The first book is the *Goetia*, based on a corrupted variation of the *Pseudomonarchia Daemonum*, produced by Johann Weyer, the reputed student of Agrippa. The next book is the *Theurgia-Goetia*, which contains an independent list of thirty-one spirits, seals, and conjurations that are associated with a positive magic (theurgy) and demonic magic (goetic), although the author doesn't make it clear which spirits belong to which classification. (The order of the spirits appears to represent some kind of element-, planetary-, and zodiacal-based magic. The third book is the *Art of Paul*, or the *Pauline Books*, consisting of two sections, the first representing a list of the angels of the hours and the second, the angels of the 360 degrees of the zodiac. The fourth book is the *Almadel* (a likely fifteenth-century grimoire by itself), which is a system of scrying magic that uses an al-madel tool or a square magical wax tablet (with a golden seal in its center) held up by wax feet and surrounded by illuminating candles at each corner. Holes in the tablet are used to allow smoke from a small brazier placed underneath the tool. The illuminated and fumigated magic square is then used as the focal point for magical operations. The last book is the *Ars Notoria* or (the *Notary Art*). This is actually a much older grimoire from the late middle ages, taken from a later sixteenth-century published version. The original versions consisted of magical psalms in a magical language arranged into intricate talismanic designs. The later published edition only had the magical words, and that is what was incorporated into the fifth book of the *Lesser Key*.

Of these five books, I have made the most extensive use of the *Goetia*, *Theurgia-Goetia*, *Ars Notoria*, and to a lesser extent, the *Greater Key of Solomon*. The *verba ignota* found in the Ars Notaria is quite powerful and very useful. The spirit lists for the first two books of the *Lesser Key* (*Goetia* and *Theurgia-Goetia*) are also quite important. So are the magic seals for these various spirits, which are to be found in these books.

Book of Abramelin the Mage—This book describes the regimen of a six- to eighteen-month spiritual retreat in order to achieve the sanctity to gain the knowledge and conversation with one's Holy Guardian Angel (HGA).

This grimoire was originally a part of the magical art of European Jews adapted for Christian magicians. The source of this book is the fourteenth-century town of Wurms, Germany, which had the oldest synagogue in Europe and a large population of Jews. The author of this grimoire was a man who called himself Abraham of Worms, but the history that he presents in the early chapters is likely spurious.

Essentially, the core operation in this book is the famous fasting, prayers, and retirement from all social activities for a period of three to six months, depending on the version of the book. It is through this period of purification and deep religious piety that the operator would gain the knowledge and conversation (known as the K & C) with his Holy Guardian Angel (HGA), and thereby reveal all of the secrets of magic. The primary goal for this achievement was to gain mastery over a group of Goetic demons and to command them to achieve whatever desires the magician put to them. There are also a collection of peculiar magical squares in the later section of the book that can only be activated by the combination of the HGA and the demons it commands.

The nearly impossible rigors of this operation has made it quite famous and fashionable for ceremonial magicians to claim having successfully achieved it. Aleister Crowley reportedly failed to complete this operation, but others in the present time have made it a kind of merit badge for the elite of ceremonial magicians. Some have lauded this grimoire and its primary ordeal, and others have declared it to be of dubious value. This ordeal is quite difficult in the modern age because few can afford to retire from the world for three to six months in order to pursue a period of exalted religious piety. Still, the most attractive and compelling part of this grimoire are the many magical squares. Yet these are considered useless and inactive unless one has gained the K & C of the HGA to activate them.

Three Books of Occult Philosophy by Henry Cornelius Agrippa—These three books were published in 1531, but later recanted by Agrippa just prior to his death in 1533. His books have remained at the pinnacle of the various writings about occult matters and magic in general because they encapsulated the basic premises of Renaissance magic as promoted by the Italian mages Ficino, Pico della Mirandola, and others. These books contain various treatises on natural or elemental magic, planetary magic, zodiacal and celestial magic, and the magic of the Qabalah. However, these books did not contain any of the rituals or practices necessary for the performance of magic, but instead they contained the foundational occult information that made such magic possible.

Another book in this series is called the *Fourth Book of Occult Philosophy*, and this book contained the specific operations needed to evoke spirits, particularly demons. While the three books of *Occult Philosophy* are readily identifiable as having been penned by Agrippa, the fourth book is of questionable origin.

However, the fourth book is quite useful because it has a copy of the Heptameron included in the appendix.[55] The Heptameron is an older grimoire, possibly from the late fifteenth century, that was the prototype for many other later grimoires.

It is a grimoire that is focused almost entirely on the invocation of angels associated with the hours and the planetary days. The invocation texts have been appropriated for other grimoires, particularly the ones associated with the evoking of demons.

It is my opinion that if someone wanted to adopt a Renaissance methodology for practicing ceremonial magic, then all four of Agrippa's books would likely be the best resource.

---

55 The *Fourth Book of Occult Philosophy* is also known as *Le Grande Albert*, as opposed to the lesser known grimoire called *Petit Albert*.

Liber Juratus a.k.a. the *Sworn Book of Honorius*—One of the oldest existing grimoires in the European Christian tradition of magic, it was likely produced in the late twelfth to early thirteenth century. Unlike other and later grimoires, *Liber Juratus* was used as a kind of magical psalter and prayer book that allowed the Catholic Mass to be secretly used to produce magical effects for the individual operator. The *Ars Notoria* was also similarly designed as a magical psalter, and was likely conceived around the same time and location. There is an ordeal rite called the beatification that has certain theurgic qualities, but mostly, this grimoire was used as magic adjunct to a pious Catholic adherence to religious liturgy, which allowed religious rituals to be adapted for magical purposes. Another curious thing about this grimoire is that it contains a magic talisman that is almost identical to the *Sigilum Aemeth* used by John Dee in his Enochian magic.

While the rituals and other workings in this grimoire are not particularly useful because they are based on Catholic liturgy, I have found the *verba ignota* written in the various psalms to be extremely powerful. I believe that this language is even more powerful than Enochian. The magical language found in this grimoire is very similar to that found in the *Ars Notoria*.

Enochian Diaries of Dr. John Dee—Perhaps the most enduring legacy that has kept Dr. John Dee in the popular imagination are the various diaries he kept filled with the notes from his various scrying sessions with his seer, Edward Kelly. These diaries are filled with the descriptions and detailed information on a comprehensive magical system that is now called Enochian magic. Dee never intended for these diaries to be preserved and published after his death, but that is exactly what happened. Later magicians, like Elias Ashmole (mid seventeenth century) attempted to organize this system, but it wasn't until the Golden Dawn and Aleister Crowley that the first attempts to make a workable system of magic from the diary contents occurred.

Since that time, there have been many books published about this system of magic, and recently, a fully realized system of magic has been derived from the diaries. Dee's magic is heavy on scrying and weak on ritualizing. He seemed to eschew many of the forms of ceremonial magic practiced in the sixteenth century, although he doubtlessly knew about them all. Dee's approach to magic was based on a very pious religious rectitude that he never abandoned nor deviated from.

I have found these many books and writings published about the contents of the Dee diaries to be very important and useful to my own work. The fact that I have used the Enochian Keys or Calls for many years as well as working with a number of the spirits (Elementals and Talismanic Elements) in that system's hierarchy have made them very valuable to me. Of course, I had to develop magical rituals to perform elemental and planetary magic in order to take advantage of these Enochian spirit lists and the associated Enochian Keys.

Arbatel—The *Arbatel* is one of the real gems in the collection of magical grimoires. It was published in 1575 by an unknown author, although some have speculated that it was originally written by Paracelsus and only published years after his death. It is also likely that the book was published by one of Paracelsus's students. This book contains forty-nine aphorisms that discuss the various philosophies and practices of a form of sacred planetary magic, incorporating the names and seals of the seven Olympian spirits. These seven demigod-like spirits are not related to any known classical sources, but rule over a total of 196 provinces that represent the universe of planetary intelligences. Each of the number of provinces that one of the Olympians rules over is sliding scale divisible by 7. Thus Aratron rules over 49, Bethor, 42, Phaleg, 35, etc. Therefore, this grimoire is a system of planetary magic, but it is very different from what is presented in Agrippa's work.

I would have to rate this grimoire as being very important because it is so succinct and unusual. As a Pagan or a Witch, you will find that summoning demigods such as the Olympian spirits will be more meaningful than the planetary spirits and angels. You can incorporate the hexagram or the septagram symbolic device in your magical workings and build a ritual-based magical system that uses them. However, the book by itself can instruct anyone to work planetary magic in a simple and direct manner

Picatrix—Only recently translated fully into English, the *Picatrix* is an early Arabic medieval grimoire that is a useful resource for astrological magic. The original title of this book was *gayar al-hakim*, or *The Aim of the Sage*. It was likely written in the eleventh century in Andalusian Spain, and it was based on earlier techniques of planetary and zodiacal magic found in late Hellenistic writings. The *Picatrix* is primarily a system of talismanic magic using a passive approach to charge talismans with subtle influences of the celestial spheres.

I have found the systems of the lunar mansions and the zodiacal decans from this work to be most useful in my own talismanic and evocation workings. Much of the other spell work is antiquated and would not be particularly useful to modern practitioners.

Greek Magical Papyri in Translation edited by Hans Dieter Betz—One of largest collection of magical rites and spells from the second century C.E. Greco-Roman Egypt. This is a massive and unique collection of magical rituals and spells. While most of the spells were written in Koine Greek, some of them were also written in Coptic and Demotic Egyptian. The assortment of rituals, the vastness of this collection, is so important because it shows us how magic was understood, perceived, and practiced in late antiquity. (There is no other collection that is as large or comprehensive.) It also contains fragments of a few of the Pagan mysteries (now long gone). While the spells might not be very useful to the modern practitioner, many of the accompanying words of power are very effective even to this day.

Sixth and Seventh Books of Moses—This is a late yet very influential grimoire that incorporates psalms, specialized seals, and magical words of power to present a kind of pseudo Jewish and supposedly Talmudic system of magic. The myth underlying this grimoire is that it contains the various magic spells and artifices used by Moses to combat the court magicians of Egypt and help him to lead his people to the Promised Land. This grimoire was likely produced from various pamphlets in Germany during the eighteenth century, but wasn't assembled into a coherent body of work until a folklorist published them in a book in 1848. Until recently, the versions in print in English were terribly garbled and contained many typos and transcription errors. Just recently, Joseph Peterson published a version of this grimoire that used the original source material, and the version that he produced is one that is free of errors and typos, revealing an impressive system of magic. However, despite the corrupted version in print, this book was widely disseminated and celebrated by German immigrants, and has found its way into the culture of African-Americans and individuals living in Western Africa. It is a magical system used to cast spells and conjure spirits for a specific purpose, based on Christian spirituality with various Jewish elements appropriated or made up to give it a more antique and foreign flavor.

The language or words of power used in this grimoire are quite potent and the many seals, characters, and special lamen are very impressive. However, the system of magic relies on the magical use of various

Biblical psalms and is very Judeo-Christian in its tone, so it might not be very valuable to a Witch or Pagan.

Grimoire Armadel—One of the most curious and likely incomplete grimoires is the *Armadel*. The *Armadel* is one of the later grimoires from the early eighteenth century. It has a very curious history, having been part of a collection of confiscated books when magicians and cunning folk were rounded up and banished from Paris after alleged aborted magical assassination attempts on the life of Louis XIV. It was an obscure manuscript in the Arsenal library in Paris until Samuel Liddel MacGregor Mathers translated it to English for his initiates. It was later published, but the version of the grimoire appears likely corrupted. For one thing, the book appears to be in a reversed order, where the title page appears as the last page instead of the first, and the other pages appear to be in the reversed order as well. As a book, it contains a number of sections filled with strange-looking magical seals with dubious Christian biblical titles. There also doesn't appear to be enough material that would allow a magician to incorporate or activate these seals, but the seals alone make this grimoire attractive to magicians and have kept it in print for years.

However, the reason the *Armadel* is on this list is because it represents a lost system of magic from the Renaissance period known as the *Art of Armadel*. What is needed is an earlier and better source copy, since the one in the Paris Arsenal library is corrupt and incomplete. Historians have speculated that there is an earlier German version of this grimoire. Hopefully, it will turn up some day and someone will publish a translated version of it.

Grimoirum Verum (*True Grimoire*)—This is one of the more controversial grimoires because it is devoted exclusively to demonic magic, likely the first of a whole group of left-hand-path magical books. While some have pushed the creation date for this grimoire to the late seventeenth century, others have shown rather conclusively, that it has its origin in the very early sixteenth century, making it the precursor for the *Lemegeton*'s *Goetia*. Most of the book concerns the evocation of a specific list of sixty-nine goetic demons, with the caveat that the magician should first engage the infernal ambassador called Scirlan. While I have found that a book dedicated mostly to goetic evocation would be problematic to someone such as myself who claims to be spiritually neutral, there is a precedent for studying and using this grimoire if you are aligned to the chthonic deities and to demonolatry.

Jake Stratton Kent has maintained that this grimoire is both important and strategic in regards to evoking goetic daemons. Kent has also published a two-volume work that has supplied a much needed foundation for this grimoire and goetic evocation in general. This book series is called *Geosophia*, and I can recommend the entire series of three books (*True Grimoire* and the *Geosophia* in two volumes) for your study as you advance in your knowledge and experience with spirit conjuring. You can gain a great deal of knowledge about Goetic magic without necessarily having to become a demonolater.

Other Left-Hand Path Grimoires—In this list are the *Grande Grimoire*, *Grimoire of Pope Honorius*, the *Black Pullet*, the *Dragon Rouge*, and the recently published *Dragon Noir*. This is a catch-all category for a number of black grimoires of the left-hand path that are currently quite popular in some circles.

A century after the *True Grimoire* was produced and disseminated in the early sixteenth century, other grimoires of the left-hand path were produced. Most of these were developed in the eighteenth and nineteenth centuries and were based on the popular notion that a magician only had to engage with an infernal ambassador representing Satan or Lucifer to achieve a kind of pact or agreement in order to work fantastic types of magic and mastery over the material world for a set period of time. These grimoires skipped the whole part where the magician should command and rule the demons, and instead was temporarily given power over them by their infernal lords. Examples of this kind of magical practice can be found in Germany with the various grimoires attributed to Faust that appeared in the seventeenth century. The pronounced left-hand path tradition of magic can trace its roots to these two phenomena but the fruit of that union began to appear in the following centuries.

Chief among these grimoires was the *Grand Grimoire*, also known as the *Dragon Rouge*, or *Red Dragon*. This book contained the directions for summoning and making a pact with Lucifer Rofocale in order to activate and empower all of the various magical spells contained in this book. Without that pact, the rest of the contents of the book were pretty much useless. While the published edition had a date of 1522 and an author (Antonio Venitiana del Rabina—Anthony the Venetian Rabbi or master), it is likely that these attributes are fictional.

Similar to the *Grand Grimoire* was another grimoire entitled the *Grimoire of Pope Honorius*, not to be confused with the *Sworn Book of Honorius*. It was likely written later, perhaps in the early nineteenth century. The *Red Dragon* spawned another knockoff, known as the *Black Dragon*, or *Dragon Noir*, which was another left-hand grimoire dedicated to conjuring infernal spirits via a diabolical pact. Another grimoire with an unsavory reputation was a small book called The *Black Pullet*, whose claim to fame was the conjuration of a black pullet or hen that could lay golden eggs—also a likely early nineteenth-century work. It also had a spell for producing the ghoulish magical tool known as the Hand of Glory, a candelabra produced from the severed hand of a hanged felon.

Two other grimoires that were at least benign and not part of the left-hand path were the *Enchiridion* and the *Petite Albert*. The *Enchiridion* was a book of psalm magic that conjured angels for various positive purposes, and the *Petite Albert* was a grimoire that contained natural, herbal, and Catholic-based magic. It was called the Petite Albert because it was written by one Alberti Parvi Lucii, which was easily confused with the great medieval sage Albertus Magnus. Being the lesser book, it was given the prefix *petite*, meaning small or lesser. Another book was called the *Grand Albert*, and this book was based on a manuscript written about natural magic also supposedly by Albertus Magnus. These books were written in the French language and represented a popular and widespread use of magic for positive or benign purposes. They were mass-produced on cheap paper and cardboard pamphlets; thousands of copies were sold.

A series of magical books that were ascribed to the secret teachings of St. Cyprian were very popular and widespread amongst the Portuguese-speaking people. The story of St. Cyprian is that he was a magician who converted to Christianity because of the empowered piety and steadfastness of a beautiful young Christian woman he attempted to magically seduce. Of course, someone who had converted to Christianity in this way would not have had any recourse to his previous sorcerous past, but he became something of a popular saint of ceremonial magic in later times, much to the chagrin of the Catholic Church. However, a complete system of magic was associated with him, and much of it concerned Goetic evocation and the commanding of demons. This represented another branch of Goetic magic that probably had as its source the *True Grimoire*, and found its way into the Americas, particularly Brazil. *The Book of St. Cyprian*, the primary source grimoire associated with this saint, was likely produced in the late eighteenth century, although it may have been later. It has influenced the magic of Palo Mayombe and also Umbanda.

That's my list of the twelve most important grimoires, and I am certain that over time you will likely develop your own list as well if you choose to explore them as I have done. As you can see, it differs remarkably from what Owen Davies has written down in his article, but then again he's a historian and I am a practitioner. We are bound to disagree on just this little matter and that's quite acceptable to me. I have briefly discussed each of the twelve grimoires that I would recommend, which is actually eleven if you discount the twelfth entry as a catch-all for several grimoires. I have given you a basic idea of what is valuable and important with each of these books. Below is a list of published materials I would recommend that you optionally purchase over time to enrich the magical system that you already possess. (Notice that most of the publishing dates are quite recent.)

Grimoires: A History of Magic Books. Owen Davies, Oxford University Press, 2009.

Veritable Key of Solomon (Sourceworks of Ceremonial Magic vol. 4). Dr. Stephen Skinner and David Rankine, Golden Hoard Press, 2008.

The Goetia of Dr. Rudd (Sourceworks of Ceremonial Magic). Dr. Stephen Skinner and David Rankine, Golden Hoard Press, 2010.

The Lesser Key of Solomon. Joseph H. Peterson, ed., Weiser Books, 2001.

Techniques of Solomonic Magic. Dr. Stephen Skinner, Golden Hoard Press, 2015.

Sepher Raziel: Liber Salomonis. Don Karr and Stephen Skinner, eds., Golden Hoard Press, 2010.

Three Books of Occult Philosophy. Henry Cornelius Agrippa, translated by James Freake, edited and annotated by Donald Tyson, Llewellyn Publications, 1997.

The Fourth Book of Occult Philosophy. Henry Cornelius Agrippa, edited with commentary by Stephen Skinner, Ibis Press, 2005.

Arbatel: Concerning the Magic of the Ancients. Translated, edited, and annotated by Joseph H. Peterson, Ibis Press, 2009.

The Sixth and Seventh Books of Moses. Edited by Joseph Peterson, Ibis Press, 2008.

The Book of Abramelin. Abraham of Worms, compiled and edited by Georg Dehn, translated by Steven Guth, Ibis Press, 2006.

The Grimoire of Armadel. Edited by S.L. MacGregor Mathers, introduction by William Keith, Weiser Books, 2001.

The Picatrix Liber Atratus Edition. Translated by John Michael Greer and Christopher Warnock, Lulu.com 2011.

Grimorium Verum. Edited and translated by Joseph H. Peterson, CreateSpace Publishing, 2007.

The True Grimoire—The Encyclopedia Goetica Volume One. Jake Stratton Kent, Bibliotheque Rouge, 2010.

Geosophia—The Argo of Magic—Encyclopedia Goetica Volume Two (in two books). Jake Stratton Kent, Bibliotheque Rouge, 2010.

The Testament of Cyprian the Mage—Encyclopedia Goetica Volume Three. Jake Stratton Kent, Bibliotheque Rouge, 2014.

The Book of St. Cyprian—The Sorcerer's Treasure. Translated and with commentary by Jose Leitao, Hadean Press, 2014.

The Greek Magical Papyri in Translation—Including the Demotic Spells. Edited by Hans Dieter Betz, University of Chicago Press, 1992.

Techniques of Graeco-Egyptian Magic. Dr. Stephen Skinner, Llewellyn Publications, 2014.

Important Source Books

A Dictionary of Angels Including the Fallen Angels. Gustav Davidson, Free Press, 1994.

The Dictionary of Demons: Names of the Damned. Michelle Belanger, Llewellyn Publications 2010.

The Qabalah of Aleister Crowley Including Gematria.

777 And Other Qabalistic Writings of Aleister Crowley: Including Gematria & Sepher Sephiroth, Weiser Books, 1986.

The Complete Magician's Tables. Dr. Stephen Skinner, Llewellyn Publications, 2006.

If you want to explore the world of grimoires on the Internet for free, Joseph H. Peterson has put together a great website with quite a lot of occult, esoteric, and also magical grimoire-based documents you can examine and download. The website is called **Esoteric Archives**, and you can find it at this address: esotericarchives.com/index.html.

Bibliography

Ankarloo, Bengt, and Stewart Clark. *Witchcraft and Magic in Europe: Ancient Greece and Rome*. London: The Athlone Press, 1999.

Betz, Hans Dieter (editor). *The Greek Magical Papyri in Translation— Including the Demotic Spells*. Chicago: University of Chicago Press, 1992.

Bremmer, Jan N., and Jan R. Veenstra (editors). *The Metamorphosis of Magic: From Late Antiquity to the Early Modern Period*. Dudley, MA: Peeters, 2002.

Crowley, Aleister. *777 and Other Qabalistic Writings of Aleister Crowley*. York Beach, ME: Samuel Weiser, 1994.

———. *The Book of Goetia of Solomon the King*. London: The Equinox Booksellers and Publishers, 1976.

———. *The Book of Thoth*. New York: Samuel Weiser, 1972.

Davidson, Gustav. *A Dictionary of Angels*. New York: Free Press, 1971.

Eliade, Mircea. *Shamanism: Archaic Techniques of Ecstasy*. Princeton, NJ: Princeton University Press, 1992.

Jackson, Nigel. *Celestial Magic: Principles and Practices of the Talismanic Art*. Milverton, UK: Capall Bann Publishing, 2003.

Jones, Alexander (editor). *The Jerusalem Bible: Reader's Edition*. Garden City, NY: Doubleday and Company, 1968.

Mathers, S. L. MacGregor. *The Grimoire of Armadel* with introduction by William Keith. New York: Weiser, 2001.

Nickelsburg, George W. E., and James C. VanderKam. *1 Enoch: A New Translation*. Minneapolis, MN: Fortress Press, 2004.

Ogden, Daniel. *Greek and Roman Necromancy*. Princeton, NJ: Princeton University Press, 2001.

Peterson, Joseph H. *Grimorium Verum: A Handbook of Black Magic*. Scotts Valley, CA: CreateSpace Publishing, 2007.

———. *The Lesser Key of Solomon*. York Beach, ME: Weiser, 2001.

Rudhyar, Dane. *The Lunation Cycle: A Key to Understanding of Personality*. New York: Aurora Press, 1986.

Skinner, Stephen. *The Fourth Book of Occult Philosophy by Henry Cornelius Agrippa*, edited with commentary. Berwick, ME: Ibis Press, 2005.

———. *Techniques of Graeco-Egyptian Magic*. Woodbury, MN: Llewellyn Publications, 2014.

Skinner, Stephen, and David Rankine. *The Goetia of Dr. Rudd (Sourceworks of Ceremonial Magic)*. Woodbury, MN: Llewellyn Publications, 2010.

———. *The Veritable Key of Solomon (Sourceworks of Ceremonial Magic)*. London: Golden Hoard Press, 2010.

————. *Veritable Key of Solomon (Sourceworks of Ceremonial Magic vol. 4)*. Woodbury, MN: Llewellyn Publications, 2008.

Smith, Morton. *Jesus the Magician*. New York: Harper and Row, 1978.

Wilbey, Emma. *Cunning Folk and Familiar Spirits: Shamanistic Visionary Traditions in Early Modern British Witchcraft and Magic*. Portland, OR: Sussex Academic Press, 2005.

Index

The Temple of High Witchcraft
Ceremonies, Spheres and The Witches' Qabalah
CHRISTOPHER PENCZAK

The Craft meets high magick in *The Temple of High Witchcraft*, the much-anticipated fourth volume in Christopher Penczak's award-winning series of Witchcraft teachings.

Penczak invites Witches to continue their spiritual evolution by exploring the ceremonial arts. Learn how these two traditions intersect in history and modern magickal practice. Penczak introduces Qabalah and discusses each sphere of the Tree of Life, in addition to ritual, pathworking, and other important concepts. In twelve lessons, you'll discover how to integrate these ideas and practices into your Craft. Following the traditional year and a day timeframe, this training program culminates with creating your own "reality map" of spiritual experience and truths.

978-0-7387-1165-2, 576 pp., 7½ x 9⅛   **$24.99**

To order, call 1-877-NEW-WRLD
Prices subject to change without notice
Order at Llewellyn.com 24 hours a day, 7 days a week